WRAPPING UP LOOSE ENDS

WRAPPING UP LOOSE ENDS

8 Simple Action Steps to
Organize Your Life Details,
Protect Your Family,
& Leave a Positive Legacy

NANCY WILLIAMSON
ATTORNEY AT LAW

102 Persian Drive, Suite 204
Sunnyvale, CA 94089

www.wrappinguplooseends.com
Copyright © 2022 Nancy Williamson
All rights reserved.
Cover and interior design by Lance Buckley.

Wrapping Up Loose Ends
8 Simple Action Steps to Organize Your Life Details, Protect Your Family, & Leave a Positive Legacy

ISBN 978-1-7369659-1-7 Paperback
        978-1-7369659-2-4 Ebook

LIBRARY OF CONGRESS CATALOGING-IN-PUBLICATION DATA

DEDICATION

This book is dedicated to those who strive to make positive changes for themselves and their loved ones.

CONTENTS

Introduction	1
Note to the Reader	11
The *Wrapping Up Loose Ends* Framework	13
Step 1: Organize Your Family's Vital Records	25
Step 2: Review Your Estate Planning Documents	41
Step 3: Organize Your Financial Information	77
Step 4: Organize Your Current Healthcare Information	117
Step 5: Document Your Future Healthcare Decisions	131
Step 6: Prepare and Plan for Your Final Wishes	147
Step 7: Create a Family Archive and Leave a Lasting Legacy	167
Step 8: Prepare an Emergency Plan and Gather Supplies	185
Wrapping Up Loose Ends: Continuing the Journey	203
Acknowledgments	209
About the Author	213

INTRODUCTION

Lives change in a moment – often without warning. During these moments of crisis, it is common for people to ask themselves in a panic what loose ends they may have. Loose ends are the unfinished strands of your life. The loose ends described in this book concern the most intimate and personal details of your life. When you leave loose ends it causes chaos, confusion, and uncertainty for your family and loved ones on top of the sadness they are already bearing. It also forces them to speculate about what you would or would not want under particular circumstances. The purpose of this book is to provide guidance on how to wrap up these loose ends and protect your family from both the expected and the unexpected.

While we all know that we will die someday, not all events can be predicted. Accidents, natural disasters, or untimely medical illness come when least expected and can cause additional havoc – but there are ways to properly plan for some contingencies.

This book provides the information and framework you need to organize these life details, separated into eight actionable steps. These steps will guide you through the process of organizing your vital records, estate planning documents, financial-planning records, current healthcare information, future healthcare decisions, final wishes, family archives, and emergency plan.

As an estate planning attorney, I know firsthand the necessity of these steps, but this book was also born out of my personal experience. When I lost three of the most important people in my life, I remember the destabilizing sense of being hit by grief, depression, and shock all at once. On top of these highly charged emotions, I was faced with looming uncertainties. My parents and my sister had never discussed death. We had no idea what any of them would want. This led to family members and friends speculating, sometimes with conflicting ideas. I went through this type of pain three times, and each time it was emotionally exhausting. This uncertainty combined with extreme grief is a recipe for disaster.

The same is true for my clients. I see too many families struggling with these same difficulties. Families and loved ones are forced to hunt down information and documents while making a myriad of decisions. All too often, the person they lost never prepared or organized these life details, and their loved ones are left to pick up the pieces. The unfortunate reality is that many families are forced to grapple with overwhelming grief and sadness while simultaneously trying to sort out these loose ends. But this additional pressure is unnecessary – and you can easily prevent it by following the eight steps outlined in this book.

That was the *aha* moment for the creation of this book. After meeting with so many families who were suffering and remembering my own family's struggles, I created an easy-to-follow roadmap so you can ensure that your families and loved ones won't have to agonize over these loose ends. And by organizing these crucial details now, you will create more serenity in your own life with the knowledge that when a death or illness does occur, your family will experience less stress knowing that your personal records have been organized and you have pre-planned your most important life decisions.

Oftentimes, clients tell me that they are not old and do not need to plan or organize these life details yet, but I wholeheartedly disagree!

Everyone over the age of eighteen should wrap up their loose ends. This is true regardless of your age. Lives are like seasons: we all have a spring, summer, fall, and winter. In our twenties and thirties, the spring of our lives, everything is fresh and new and full of promise. The world is full of possibilities and excitement. We are embarking on our careers, interests, and family choices. Some are exploring career options, having children, or buying their first home. Some are traveling the globe. Spring is typically the time when we are finding ourselves and determining our place in the world.

In our forties and fifties, the summer of our lives, we tend to be more established. We are secure in our careers and are growing and developing in our chosen professions. Many have children who are young adults as well as aging parents, and are simultaneously planning for their own retirement. For most, life is settled and we are concentrated on accumulating wealth and life experiences.

In our sixties and seventies, the autumn of our lives, we may be transitioning into a second career or retirement. Many have children, and their children are older and may be starting families of their own. Nowadays, with increasing life expectancy, things have shifted and some life events are happening at later seasons. These are merely examples.

In the winter of our lives, which is in our eighties and above, health concerns are typically more prevalent. We may be concerned about future healthcare, living expenses, long-term-care expenses, and leaving a legacy.

Each of these seasons presents a unique set of pleasures and joys, as well as particular needs and concerns. Each person transitions through seasons in their own unique way, and have their own needs, challenges, and goals. The eight steps in this book apply to everyone, regardless of your age. However, depending on your season of life, some parts of the steps may be more relevant to you.

As an estate planning attorney, I have the pleasure and honor of creating estate planning documents for clients in each season of life. Most of these concerns relate to financial well-being, estate planning, healthcare concerns, and leaving a legacy. This book provides a framework for addressing these eight essential life details. Each section will start by discussing the basic overview of and concepts behind that particular step.

During the completion of each step, you will explore four basic questions.

The first is your *Why*: Why do I need to organize this information and these documents? Why is it important?

The second is your *What*: What do I need to organize?

The third is your *Where*: Where should I keep this information?

The fourth is your *How*: How I should manage this information?

You may have noticed that I am missing one of the common elements – *when*. Now, you may ask yourself, *why did she leave that out?* I left that out because the time to complete these eight steps is now!

If you're like me, you may get excited at the prospect of a new project but then let it fall by the wayside. I recommend setting a deadline for completing this book, and I encourage you to read and complete each step within a predetermined timeframe. I like to divide the process of each step up into three weeks. Each week, schedule time to complete two or three of the tasks required. In addition, I encourage you to set reminders to keep you on track.

Another good technique is to use an accountability partner. I would wager that you have been thinking about organizing these details, or "putting your affairs in order," or "getting your ducks in a row" for a long time. An accountability partner keeps you both on track. You can set deadlines and check in with each other to record your progress. When you finish a section, do not forget to take time to celebrate and congratulate each other on your progress. Upon the completion of each step, you are moving closer to the goal of organizing your life details, protecting your family, and leaving a lasting legacy.

I also recommend that you review the documents and information annually on a predetermined date. A good method is to pick a date that is associated with starting fresh, such as a few days before or after your birthday, at the beginning of the year, or when you are completing your taxes. It is a good idea to place your review date on your calendar and complete it as a yearly tradition. For example, many of my clients review this information in January of each year. When reviewing each of the eight steps, you should update information and add in any new pertinent documents or items.

It is also advisable to update as major life changes occur. For example, if you have a child or get married, you will want to update the information and documents for each step. As your life changes, this organizational system should keep pace with you. The good news is that once you have an established system, it is much easier to update your information and documents.

Regardless of your season of life or how long you've been intending to get organized, this is not an activity for tomorrow, next week, or next year. The time is now! Procrastination is easy but action is difficult. The time to take control is now! Let's get started!

NOTE TO THE READER

This book is based on my experiences as an estate planning attorney. Stories and examples have been included to illustrate some of the concepts.

This book is not intended to be legal advice, nor is there any expectation that an attorney–client relationship has been formed.

My office is located in California, so some of the names of the government offices I reference may have a different name in the area where you live. Throughout this book, I have attempted to use general names and terms.

The *Wrapping Up Loose Ends* Framework

The purpose of this book is to provide you with a clear framework and action plan. Each step is divided into manageable tasks. At the completion of this book, you will have confidence that your loved ones will have all of the information they need, and there are no loose ends.

Each step will pose four questions:

1. Why do I need to organize this information?

2. What do I need to organize?

3. Where should I keep the information and documents?

4. How should I manage the information and documents?

Let's begin with the first and most important question – the *why*. This is the reason and motivation for taking the time to review and organize the information outlined in this book. The *why* is the easiest question; most clients agree that each of these steps are important. In order to keep yourself motivated, you may want to identify your specific *why* before beginning a new step. Most of my clients identify their *why* as not wanting to cause additional grief for their loved ones after they die, so this is the reason they want to complete these steps. For additional motivation, you may want to imagine the consequences of not completing a step.

The second question pertains to the *what*. These are the types of documents you will want to organize. Under each category of documents is basic information about each type of document. There can sometimes be confusion regarding the purpose and function of various documents, so I've provided a brief explanation for easy reference. Of course, this is not an in-depth review of each document, and I encourage you to consult a professional when needed.

The last two questions are the *how* and the *where*. These questions are interrelated. The *how* and *where* concern whether you are going to manage this information digitally, on paper, or both. I am frequently asked by my clients what methods should be utilized. The answer to this question depends on personal preferences. There are pros and cons to both. If you only have paper documents, these documents can be easily misplaced or lost; I often get calls from clients who have moved and cannot find their estate planning binder, for instance. Having a digital copy can be handy, but of course there are risks with this method as well; for example, what if your computer is hacked and these documents are accessed? There is no easy answer. It's for you to decide what is best for you and what makes you feel comfortable. In the next section, we will review some of the options and their practical considerations.

First, let's start with paper documents. While many of my clients have most of their documents saved digitally, many maintain paper documents as well. It's easy for paper documents to get out of control and end up in disorganized stacks in our homes and offices. Oftentimes when I meet with clients for the first time, they arrive with a shopping bag or a box containing stacks of envelopes and documents. As I ask them questions, they shuffle through these documents searching for the requested information. I can sense their frustration as they struggle to find information and the needed document. Having to spend countless hours looking for documents and information is frustrating and a waste of time. It is even more difficult after the death of your loved one to locate the required documents and information, if it is not well organized. This book is designed to solve this problem and show you how to take control of your documents.

In my opinion, a well-organized filing cabinet is a crucial part of this process. The information in each section of this book should have a place in your filing system. For example, for your vital records, you will have multiple files that contain the documents outlined in that section. This same process should be completed for each of the steps.

I find that folders are the best way to organize paper documents. I choose high-quality pressboard folders for my files. These are particularly useful because they'll last longer than other types of folders. Each folder should be labeled; this is an important part of the process. A great investment is a label-maker or sheets of labels so you can print specific labels for each item. As the years go by, labels tend to fall off and fade, so I recommend that you secure them with some clear packing tape. This keeps them in place for years and prevents discoloration. I often make two labels, place one on the front and one on the back, and secure both sides with tape.

While I personally prefer file folders, there are a myriad of other options. Some clients prefer binders or expandable folders. Another option is to create binders that contain a divider for each step. Under each tab, you can include sub-sections for the various types of information and documents. You may choose to use an accordion-file system in which you create a divider for each step and file the appropriate documents under clearly labeled sub-tabs. There is no one-size-fits-all solution, and these are just some examples. What is appropriate depends on your personal preference; you should pick the type of system that works best for you and allows you to easily add new documents and information.

As you work through each step, you will create a stack of folders or several binders. The next question is: what will happen if you need information in an emergency? For example, what if there's a situation requiring you to evacuate your home? Or what if there's a situation where your loved one is in the hospital, and you need his or her advance healthcare directive?

For this reason, I suggest also creating an essential-information file. This is a separate accordion file (or other type of binder or folders) that you can grab in case of an emergency. Whatever storage method you choose, make sure that it's easy to transport. You should plan for possible emergencies in advance; make sure your family knows the location of this file and has instructions to take it in case of an emergency. Step 8 reviews the things you'll want to consider when planning for an emergency.

Your essential information file should include at least eight tabs, one for each of the steps. In each tab, you should place physical copies of the most important documents and information. For example, tab one would be titled Vital Records, and would include your original passport and a copy, a copy of your driver's license, and your original social security card. You may even want to include a flash drive with electronic copies of the documents, and instructions on how to access the cloud if you store documents there. This process should be completed for each step. Later in this chapter, we will discuss digitizing documents. This is an important part of the process because you will have a file that is easy to transport if an emergency arises.

If there is an evacuation order, typically you do not have much time to gather documents. You may only have fifteen minutes or so to gather the essentials. Having this pre-planned and ready to go will go a long way toward creating peace of mind.

Contact List

With the advent of the cell phone, many people do not have physical address books. It is convenient to have all of your contacts in your phone, but what if your phone has a passcode and your loved ones don't know how to access it? How would they know whom you would want contacted if you are incapacitated or deceased? Or what if your phone breaks and you are unable to access your contacts?

This is why I suggest that you back up your phone on a regular basis, and keep a contact list. This may include contact information for professionals and service providers, such as your doctors, lawyers, financial advisors, and insurance agents, just to name a few.

It may also include information about your trustees, agents for powers of attorney, and contact information for your beneficiaries. Additionally, you may want to include the contact information for your social circle. This will give your loved ones access to the contact information for relatives, friends, and associates you would like contacted if you become incapacitated or when you die. It is important to update this contact information when it changes.

A current contact list should also be included in your filing system, as well as in your essential information kit. This contact list can be as detailed as your like, and can include instructions on whom to contact, when, and under what circumstances.

Purging

Purging documents can be one of the most difficult tasks for many of my clients. It is human nature to want to keep all papers; however, it is important to keep your files relevant and up-to-date. You should regularly review your documents and determine if any can be purged.

With that being said, there are sentimental papers and documents that you may wish to preserve in paper format for your lifetime and pass onto future generations. This will be discussed later, in Step 7 – Family Archives.

Digitizing Your Documents

Nowadays, it is much easier to digitize documents. With the increase of memory space on computers and the improvement of scanners, it much simpler and faster to scan and store documents.

There are now numerous options for storing documents and information. You may use a flash drive, the cloud, or document-management software. With advancing technology, there are many options available, and there will be new options in the future. Which system or combination of systems you will want to use depends on your preferences and comfort level. As we move through each step, you will want to create a plan for how and where to store your documents.

Now that we have reviewed the four questions, let's move on to Step 1!

☑ CHECKLIST

1. Choose an organization method

2. Create an essential-information kit

3. Contact list

    a. Back up your cell phone regularly

    b. Prepare a list of contacts with instructions for whom you would like to be contacted and under what circumstances. You may want to include contact information for family, friends, professionals, trustees, and beneficiaries.

4. Keep this information up-to-date. Review this information on an annual basis, and make changes as needed.

STEP 1

Organize Your Family's Vital Records

Vital records are the lifeblood of your identity. They are the official proof of your birth, marriage, and other life events. These are the documents that future generations will use to gather genealogical information. Organizing them and having a place to store them will ensure that vital records are easy to find and readily accessible when needed. Vital records should be gathered and organized for each family member.

The following pages list vital records organized by their type, either identification documents or documents related to life events. This list is not meant to be exhaustive. Some may be relevant to your life circumstance, others may not. This is merely a guide you can use to help you to form a checklist of records you should organize.

IDENTIFICATION DOCUMENTS

First, let's start with identification documents. Identification documents are those documents that prove birth and citizenship. In the following section, some of the major documents are outlined.

Birth Certificate

For each family member, you should keep a certified copy of his or her birth certificate. An official, certified copy will typically be multi-colored and embossed or stamped with a seal. You should verify that you have the original plus a copy for each member of your family. You may also want to scan and digitally store it.

Driver's License or State-Issued Identification

For each family member, obtain a copy of his or her driver's license or state-issued identification card. If you have a child who is not driving yet, obtain a current copy of his or her school identification card and/or driver's permit.

Passport

Keep the original passport plus a copy for each family member.

Social Security Card

Keep the original social security card plus a copy for each family member.

HOW TO MANAGE YOUR IDENTIFICATION DOCUMENTS

I recommend placing these originals and copies in your preferred organizational system, whether it's a binder or a filing cabinet. Keep in mind that some identification documents, such as the driver's license and passport, expire at various times. In order to manage these renewal dates, I suggest that you keep the following list for your identification documents.

- Social security card
    - Social security number
    - The exact way the name appears on the card

- Driver's license
    - Driver's license number
    - The exact way the name appears on the card
    - Renewal date
    - Any restrictions?
    - Is there an organ-donation preference noted on the license?

- Passport and passport card
    - How the name appears on the passport
    - Passport number
    - Expiration date

Since this is sensitive information, you will want to ensure that this information is properly secured.

DOCUMENTS RELATED TO MAJOR LIFE EVENTS

Marriage Certificate

This folder should contain a certified copy of your marriage certificate.

Immigration Documents

If you have immigrated, you should keep all records related to the application as well as copies of your green card, and naturalization certificate, if applicable.

Dissolution Documents

If you are divorced or legally separated, it is important to keep copies of these documents. While it may be tempting to throw them away, you should keep in mind that these documents may be necessary in the future. For example, a copy of your Judgment of Dissolution may be required before you can apply for the social security benefits or pension benefits of a former spouse.

While in line at court, I am often a witness to the frustration of the person ahead of me when they realize they don't have the case number. If the dissolution information was digitized and is in the online system, it is easily located. However, if the dissolution occurred decades earlier, it can be a challenge to locate the case number, and may require extensive research.

I have also been in line at court when someone realizes that they never filed their Final Judgment of Dissolution, and are still married to the spouse they thought they had divorced. This is particularly awkward if the second spouse is at the court and has just realized that their spouse was already married when they exchanged wedding vows.

It is a good idea to locate your final Judgment of Dissolution and place it in your Vital Records file. If you need this document in the future, having this information will save you time. There are a myriad of reasons why you may need it; when you apply for social security or other types of benefits, for example, the government agency may require a copy.

Also keep in mind that in the future, you may need a certified copy of the Judgment of Dissolution. A certified copy of a court document is stamped and signed by the court clerk verifying that this is a true and correct copy of the document. The certified copy is requested from the court where the divorce was obtained. If you already have the case number and the date of the Judgment of Dissolution, you can simply request a certified copy. The court clerk can easily locate the file because you have provided the necessary information. There is an additional charge for the certified copy, so you'll want to check first whether a certified copy is required.

Name-Change Documents and/or Gender-Change Documents

If you have filed a petition for name change or gender change, you should keep a copy of the petition, the supporting documents, and a copy of the order changing name and/or gender. This is another type of document where you may need additional certified copies to provide to government agencies. It makes it much simpler if you already have the case number and the date of the order when you are requesting certified copies of the order from the court.

Death Certificates

When a loved one dies, you will want to keep an original certified copy of the death certificate in your Vital Records folder. When you are making final arrangements, you will be asked by the mortuary how many certified copies you want to order. The number you need depends on the number of assets the decedent owned. Clients will come into my office with a stack of twenty. In many cases, you may only require five or ten. When you are administering the estate and submitting death certificates to institutions for their review, you can request that they return the original certified copies to you when they are done.

Also keep in mind that if you require additional death certificates, you can always obtain additional ones from the county office that manages vital records in the county where your loved one died.

Obtaining Duplicate Copies

There may be vital records that are relevant to you but that you are unable to find. This is a good time to obtain a duplicate copy for your files. This process will depend on the type of document and the government agency where the records are stored. For example, you may just need to research this on the website of the county where the life event occurred. Each county will have a department that manages these records; it may be called the Department of Vital Records or some other similar name.

When you order a birth or death certificate, the entity will need to verify that you are entitled to a copy. They will ask for your relationship to the individual or decedent.

They will then issue a certified copy. A certified copy is considered an original document because it is authenticated by the county as a true and correct copy of the record on file with the governmental agency.

Other types of documents may be obtained locally; a copy of your social security card can be requested from your local social security office, for example. Some others, such as dissolution or name-change documents, can be obtained from the court where the order was filed. Before requesting a copy, you should determine whether you need a certified copy, which will have an additional charge.

Military Documents

If you are currently in active duty or on reserve, now is the time to organize your military documents. If you are an active-duty service member, you'll want to create a folder with a copy of your military identification and enlistment documents.

If you have been discharged from the military or have retired, you will want to locate your relevant military documents. The most important document is the DD-214, which is the Honorable Discharge document. The DD-214 is required before you can apply for many military benefits. You should verify that they have a copy of this document. If you are unable to locate this document, you can obtain a duplicate copy from the United States National Archives and Records Administration.

Organizing Your Vital Information Documents

After you have located each relevant document, you may want to scan them so they will be accessible. If you decide to scan them, you will need to determine how to store them – in an email account, in the cloud, etc. However, the issue always comes back to who will have access and how best to organize them. In the previous chapter, I reviewed methods for organizing this information – either paper, electronic, or both. This is a personal decision and the methods used should be based on what works for you.

Now is the time to review and organize your vital records. This step is the first one in this book because these are the most basic and foundational of all of our life details. Along with locating these documents, you should also make a plan for how and where to store these documents.

We take these types of documents for granted, but when you need one of them and can't find it, it can be very frustrating and you may end up wasting a lot of time. I encourage you to finish this step before moving to the next one. If you need to take notes or make a to-do list, I have included an action item list at the end of the chapter for your use.

☑ STEP 1
VITAL RECORDS CHECKLIST

1. Identification Documents

    a. Birth Certificate

    b. Driver's License

    c. Passport

    d. Make a list of how your name appears on each piece of identification, the number, and the expiration date.

2. Major Life Events Documents

    a. Marriage Certificate

    b. Immigration documents

    c. Dissolution documents

    d. Name-change / gender-change documents

    e. Death Certificate

3. Military Documents

    a. If you are serving or have served in the military, gather any and all relevant documents.

4. Gather each of the vital records relevant to you. If you are unable to find any of the documents, obtain duplicate copies.

5. Create a plan for storing these documents. Remember to place the originals or copies in your essential-information file.

STEP 1 – NOTES AND ACTION ITEMS

☐ _____

☐ _____

☐ _____

☐ _____

☐ _____

☐ _____

☐ _____

☐ _____

☐ _____

STEP 2

Review Your Estate Planning Documents

Estate planning documents are your family's roadmap. It provides directions to your family for how to distribute your assets after you pass away. Your appointed decision-makers can handle all of the administration of your affairs of your estate and distribute your assets to the named beneficiaries. Additionally, a complete estate plan will include documents authorizing individuals to make health and financial decisions in the event of future incapacity. Incapacity includes dire situations such as comas or neurological conditions that prevent you from making decisions.

Having a well-planned-out roadmap is useless if your family can't access these documents. At the end of this chapter, we'll explore methods of organizing the documents and information. For the moment, let's examine what documents you will want to review and organize.

The following pages are a brief overview of the types of documents you'll need; it is not intended to be exhaustive. You will want to consult with an attorney who specializes in estate planning regarding specific questions you may have.

Beneficiary-Driven Assets

Keep in mind that assets such as your 401(k), IRA, annuities, and life insurance are distributed via the named beneficiaries. These assets are separate from the living trust or will and are distributed to your named beneficiaries upon your death. It is advisable to periodically review your named primary beneficiaries and contingent beneficiaries and confirm that these choices are consistent with your intent.

For example, what if you have named an estranged child or a former partner as your primary beneficiary? If you pass away and that person is named as the beneficiary, he or she is entitled to receive the asset, regardless of the provisions in your living trust or will. This is why it's important to periodically review your named beneficiaries.

Living Trusts and Wills

Depending on your state of residence, your estate planning documents may consist of a living trust and pour-over will or just a last will and testament. If your assets are not over your state's probate limit, then a last will and testament may be the only document required. This document names executors who administer your estate as well as specific provisions regarding distributions. Even if this is the case, you will still want to check your primary and contingent beneficiaries because these assets are distributed based on the beneficiary designation.

If your estate is above the maximum amount that can be distributed without probate in your state, then a living trust may be advisable. The living trust is a document authorizing your trustee to administer your estate without court oversite.

If you are preparing a living trust, you will need to designate a successor trustee and alternates. You'll want to ensure that your chosen trustee is fiscally responsible with his or her own finances, and that he or she has agreed to serve in this role. You may want to consider naming a primary trustee and one or two alternates.

Many parents feel guilty if they have chosen one child to serve as the first trustee and the remaining children as the successor trustees. They often tell me that they don't want to play favorites. While I know it can be difficult to choose trustees, it is my philosophy that you should choose the person best able to handle the responsibilities. It can be helpful to talk to your children about your decisions. Most adult children will be supportive and relieved that you have included them in the conversation. Of course, this is a personal decision.

Additionally, a living trust does require funding. The term funding merely means re-titling the proper assets into the name of your living trust. These include assets such as real estate, bank accounts, and brokerage accounts, just to name a few.

Along with the living trust, you will most likely have a pour-over will. The pour-over will is the backup to the trust and shows the decedent's intent about the administration of assets not titled in the living trust upon death. For example, in some states, if you pass away and property over the probate limit is not titled in the trust, the pour-over will may be used to successfully re-title this asset into the name of the living trust.

Many clients are also concerned with the distribution of their tangible possessions, such as jewelry, coin collections, artwork and other types of personal items. The pour-over will may include provisions outlining the distribution of these items.

Since these possessions are often of sentimental value, I frequently advise clients to add pictures of the items. For example, if a provision states that the ruby ring goes to Aunt Clara, you can include an attachment with a picture of the ring. You may want to provide further details about these items.

I have had a few cases where the family had difficulty dividing sentimental items. A lack of directions for how to distribute personal property can lead to conflict if the children can't agree on who will receive them. It can be a small item that causes the most grief for a family; it's usually not about the actual item but about the unresolved issues. That is why it is a good idea to have a plan for distributing the personal items and discuss the issues with your family.

Step 3 provides guidance on inventorying and insuring these items, and Step 7 offers ideas on leaving information about their significance.

Minor Children

If you have minor children, you will want to ensure that you have a guardianship provision, which names a guardian who will raise your children in the event that you pass away before your children reach the age of eighteen years old.

This is a choice that is made with your head and your heart. While there are practical considerations to take into account, there are also emotional, subjective reasons for choosing a particular guardian or set of guardians. This is one of the hardest decisions for a parent to make. When I meet with clients who have minor children, this is the most difficult discussion.

First, it feels unnatural to imagine that you would not be alive to take care of your children. The thought is inconceivable and upsetting. Regardless of these feelings, this is a crucial item for parents to plan.

The first question is whom to name. Should you name a couple or a single person? If you name a couple, what would happen if the couple were to divorce? Would you want the children to stay with one or the other? Of course, you will name primary guardians, but you should also name alternate guardians, in case the primary guardian is unable or unwilling to serve as guardian.

Then there are further considerations. Where do your proposed guardians live? How old are they? Do they have other children, and if so, do your children get along with them? Do the proposed guardians have room in their home for your children?

These are just some of the questions you will want to address, and of course you will want to discuss these issues with the proposed guardian beforehand to make sure he or she feels comfortable being named in this role.

Special Needs Children

If you have a child with special needs, it is imperative to carefully plan for him or her. Creating a special-needs trust can ensure that your child receives their portion of the inheritance without jeopardizing their public benefits. Speaking to a qualified estate planning attorney who has experience with special-needs planning will help you to set up a special-needs trust that will protect your child.

Foreign Assets

If you own property, real estate, or bank accounts abroad, you will want to determine how that property will be distributed upon your death. You'll need to consult with an attorney in that country who can advise you how to plan for these overseas assets.

Planning for Your Pets

For many clients, pets are considered part of their families. In your estate planning, you may want to include a pet trust provision. This directs your trustee to give your pet to a named individual or find a suitable home.

In 1980, there was a famous California case concerning a dog named Sido.[1] The will of Sido's owner contained a provision that when she died, Sido would be destroyed. The San Francisco SPCA fought to save the dog. As a result, California passed legislation that an animal cannot be euthanized as directed in the decedent's will.

Your local SPCA or your local animal shelter typically has a registration program. You can register your pet with them and when you pass away or if you become

---

[1] Christie Keith, "Saving Sido: How One Dog Sparked a Movement," SF Gate, June 22, 2010, https://www.sfgate.com/pets/yourwholepet/article/Saving-Sido-How-one-dog-sparked-a-movement-2463520.php.

incapacitated, they will find an appropriate home for your pets.

You will want to keep complete records for each of your pets. This will include identification information, such as the microchip number, pet license information, and adoption information. You will also want to include the name of your pet's veterinarian, vaccination records, pet insurance, and any other types of information that would be useful. If you have an emotional-support or service animal, you will want to keep separate files for each animal along with copies of the certification.

Planning for smaller animals, such as cats and dogs, is less complicated than planning for large animals, such as horses, livestock, or exotic animals. For each animal, you will want to keep a file with a picture of each animal, identification information and, veterinary records.

Regardless of the type of animals that you have, you will want to keep detailed records and files for each of them. This can be invaluable information if there is an emergency and you lose track of your animals. In Step 8, planning for animals in an emergency situation will be explored further.

Durable Power of Attorney for Finances

Estate planning also consists of planning for possible incapacity. For example, your durable power of attorney for finances names an individual (sometimes called an agent) who will handle your finances in the event you become incapacitated. This document allows this individual to pay your bills, deposit checks, and file your taxes. It is always a good idea to name a primary agent and alternates.

More often than not, this will be written as a springing document. This means that it only goes into effect if and when you become incapacitated and your condition has been verified by a physician.

Advance Healthcare Directive, or Living Will

The advance healthcare directive, or living will, names an agent and successor agents who will make medical decisions in the event of your incapacity. Similar to the durable power of attorney for finances, this document typically only goes into effect if and when you become incapacitated. A more in-depth discussion of the advance healthcare directive can be found in Step 5.

Annual Review

Once your estate planning documents are completed, it is a good idea to review them on a yearly basis. For example, you will want to review your trustee, executor, guardian, and agent provisions and confirm these are the individuals you would want to serve in these roles.

During your yearly review you should also review the distribution provisions. Do the percentages and/or specific amounts you have listed still reflect your wishes? At the end of this chapter is an Estate Planning Checklist for your use.

How to Organize These Documents

One of the most common questions clients ask me is "where should I keep this estate planning binder?" In my practice, I give the original documents to the client and keep signed and executed copies in the file and maintain a digital copy. If an attorney prepared the documents, you should inquire about their document-retention policy.

Where to Keep the Originals?

In the following section, we'll explore many options regarding the management of these documents. Estate planning documents are private and copies are not filed with the government agency upon execution, so it is crucial to have a plan for managing these documents and maintaining alternate ways to access them.

Safe-Deposit Box

While a safe-deposit box may seem like the most logical place to store your estate planning documents, there are some logistics to consider. If your trustee is not a signor on the safe-deposit box, he or she will have to produce a death certificate and perhaps other documentation, and may have to wait a certain number of days before he or she is allowed to access it.

In California, for example, forty days must have elapsed after the death, plus the trustee will need an original, certified copy of the death certificate, a copy of the trust showing that he or she is the trustee, and a key. If the trustee needs a copy of the living trust and the sole copy is located in the safe-deposit box, this can cause a whole host of problems and delays. So before placing the original estate planning documents in a safe-deposit box, you will want to carefully consider how your trustee and/or agent will gain access to the documents when needed.

One option is to add your trustee as a signor. You can give your successor trustee instructions that he or she should open the box and retrieve your estate planning documents after your death or in the event of your incapacity.

This type of access may make some individuals uncomfortable because the signor has access to your safe-deposit box, at any time. What if you change your mind about who should be your trustee or agent, and you forget to take their name off the signatory list? Before deciding on this option, you may want to consider the following ideas.

Keep the Documents at Home

Many clients decide to keep their original estate planning documents at home, in a designated drawer or filing cabinet. If you're going to store your documents at home, you will want to let your trustee and agent know where you're planning to keep them so they're easily accessible. Others opt to install a safe in their home. If you are considering purchasing a safe, there are a few considerations. Safes are rated according to whether they can withstand fire or burglary. Many are rated just for fire, meaning that they can hold up against a fire up to a certain number of degrees. Others are meant to thwart burglars, with locking bolts and steel walls designed to resist prying and drilling. You can also bolt it to the floor to discourage burglars.

Some are rated for both fire and burglary. These safes are classified with UL ratings by Underwriters Laboratories, an organization that tests the quality of safety products for use by federal and global agencies.

If you are thinking of purchasing a safe, you may want to consult a locksmith regarding which option is best for you.

Digital Copies

Some clients feel more comfortable having a physical copy and digital copy. Some keep them in their personal email account or in the cloud. Some also like to email the documents to their named successor trustees and agents, though not everyone wants to share this private information before it is needed. If you do choose to provide these documents to your trustee, you will also need to remember to provide them with any amendments.

Another option is to enlist a cloud service or document-retention service that allows access by your designated trustee or agent after a triggering event has occurred.

Most individuals have the original documents, but it is important to consider other methods in which you will manage these documents. Many clients decide to manage physical copies as well as digital copies.

Durable Power of Attorney

Most durable powers of attorney are written as springing documents, meaning that they only take effect if and when you become incapacitated and a doctor writes a letter stating that you do not have the capacity to make financial decisions.

Your agent will need the durable power of attorney if a triggering event occurs. If you are incapacitated, you will not be able to tell your agent where the document is located. You will want a system in place that allows access by the designated individual so they can pay your bills, deposit checks, and file your tax returns. This is the time to create a plan for how your agent can access this document, if needed. If you keep the only copy in a safe-deposit box, it will be difficult for your agent to access the document if it becomes necessary.

Another alternate is to keep it in your house and tell your agent where it's located. If you keep this document in a safe, you will want to provide your agent with information on how to access the safe.

You may want to email this document to your agent, if you feel comfortable. You can also decide to use a cloud-based service that would allow your agent to access the document upon subsequent incapacity.

Advance Healthcare Directive / Living Will

When it comes to your advance healthcare directive, or living will, you may want to give a copy to your primary care physician to place in your medical file. In the event of a medical emergency, your doctor can provide this document to the hospital where you're being treated.

You will also want to keep this document somewhere accessible. Similar to the durable power of attorney for finances, this is commonly a springing document, only going into effect if and when you become incapacitated.

The advance healthcare directive, or living will, is distinct from the other estate planning documents because it's a document your agent may need right away if there is a medical emergency. It will be further explored in Step 6. But for now, the question is access, especially in the case of an emergency.

There are several places you may want to consider keeping this document. As discussed earlier, you can keep it in a safe-deposit box or safe, but this can cause problems if your agent needs a copy but is unable to access the safe-deposit box or home safe. While your primary care physician may have a copy, your agent might not know the name of this doctor to request a copy.

Similar to your other estate planning documents, you may want to consider emailing this document to your named agent or utilizing a digital service that will allow access upon the occurrence of incapacity. Some states also maintain a registry where you can store your advance healthcare directive.

You may also want to download a copy of this document to your phone or tablet. You will need to remember to upload a copy to new devices. Also, whenever you update the document, you'll need to upload the latest version. You might consider keeping a copy of this document in the glove box of your car, and when you travel, you may also want to keep a copy in your suitcase, or a digital copy in the electronic device you travel with. If you are only planning to bring a digital copy, verify that your travel companions know how to access it.

Updating Documents

It's common for clients to amend their estate planning documents to keep pace with the changes in their lives. It is important to keep all versions of your documents. If you modify these documents often, it can become confusing to keep track of these changes.

At the end of this chapter is a table you can use to document the amendments; you will also want to update your digital repository. If you are using a cloud-based service, don't forget to upload the revised documents. If you are providing digital copies to your trustees/agents, don't forget to give them any revised estate planning documents. It is also important to update your digital repository, when documents are amended.

Organizing Your Digital Life

With the advent of the internet and social media, many clients own digital assets. These are assets that are electronically stored. Digital assets can include emails, photos, videos, music, movies, domain names, virtual gaming assets, travel accounts, crypto currencies, and social media accounts. In the next section, I will review organizational considerations. Many clients own hundreds of digital assets.

These types of assets are often overlooked when clients are inventorying their assets, simply because they are taken for granted. We access them every day, often multiple times, but we don't think about distribution of them or access to them upon death.

Additionally, each state has different laws pertaining to access to digital assets. Depending on where you live, you'll want to find out which laws are applicable and prepare a formal digital-estate plan.

Some of the items you may want to inventory are the assets listed below. For each of these items, you'll want to include the log-in usernames, passwords, and pin numbers (if applicable).

- Email accounts (include email address and password)
- Bank accounts
- Financial accounts, such as brokerage accounts and online stock purchasing programs
- Credit cards
- Entertainment accounts, such as movies, books, and music.
- Services that store your personal videos and photographs
- Frequent-flyer miles
- All of the digital tools used to manage your business

Given the sheer number of digital assets, this list probably does not include all of your categories. I recommend that you start preparing a list. Since it's difficult to sit down and list every digital asset from memory, I recommend that you take time each day to document the digital assets that you find yourself using. One idea is to keep a list each day for a week with the names and URLs of the websites you often access. You will want to continue cataloging these digital assets until you have accounted for all of the ones that are essential to your life and/or business.

If you do make a list of these websites, this may want to include sensitive information, such as log-ins and passwords.

If you do keep a written list, you will want to utilize a system to safeguard against unauthorized access.

These days, many clients have transitioned much of their financial life online. There are automatic deposits and bill pays linked to their bank accounts. A typical problem occurs when someone becomes incapacitated or passes away and their loved ones don't know what deposits are automatically made or which debts are on automatic pay. So I suggest you keep an updated list of these automatic deposits and payments. We'll will go into more depth about financial information in Step 3, which includes a table you can use to catalog your automatic deposits and automatic payments.

Social Media Accounts

With the popularity of social media, more and more people are regularly using these sites. For example, as of the time of the writing of this book, the Pew Research Center estimates that 68% of US adults use Facebook and 43% review news on it.[2]

Much of our lives are memorialized on social media. In the following section, I have outlined some of the most

---

[2] John Gramlich, "10 Facts About Americans and Facebook," Pew Research Center, February 1, 2019, https://www.pewresearch.org/fact-tank/2019/02/01/facts-about-americans-and-facebook/.

popular social media sites, as well as how to plan for the management of these accounts if you become incapacitated or after you pass away. Of course, it would be impossible to list each and every one. I suggest that you review the policies for each social media site you utilize and decide how you want it managed in the future.

The information contained in the following pages is based on information gathered at the time of writing this book. Policies change often, so you should verify them when completing your preferences for these social media sites.

Facebook

One of the most popular social media sites is Facebook. What would you like your heirs to do with this account after you die? Do you want your account memorialized or permanently deleted? According to Facebook, if they become aware of your passing, they will memorialize it, unless you have informed them that you wish for it to be permanently deleted.

If you have chosen to have it memorialized, you have the option of choosing a legacy contact who can post on your behalf, respond to new friend requests, and update information on your page. Additionally, the legacy contact can download everything that has been shared on Facebook. More detailed instructions can be found at the Facebook help center under the heading "Memorialized Accounts."

Instagram

On the Instagram platform, family members can memorialize the account. Before the memorialization can occur, Instagram will require proof that the individual has passed away, such as a death certificate or obituary. They will also require that the person requesting memorialization is an immediate family member. Proving this relationship will require a birth certificate showing the relationship between the parties, the death certificate, or proof that you are the personal representative of the decedent's estate.

Instagram does not allow the account to be changed. The posts of the decedent remains intact. For more information, you will want to review the policies located at the Instagram help center, under "Memorialized Accounts."

Twitter

Twitter has similar rules regarding deactivation of the account. In the event that a Twitter user has died, a family member can request the removal of the deceased user's account. However, you must prove your relationship with the decedent. This requires documentation, such as proof of your identification and a copy of the death certificate.

Similarly, Twitter also has a policy regarding the incapacitated user. The agent for the power of attorney can request that the Twitter account be deactivated, if he or she provides documentation that the Twitter user is incapacitated. This requires a copy of the power of attorney, and proof of his or her relationship to the Twitter user.

LinkedIn

After the death of a LinkedIn member, a family member can remove the profile. The requestor must provide the decedent's name, the URL to the LinkedIn profile, the relationship to the decedent, the email address, the date he or she passed away, a link to the obituary, and their employment information. This information is required pursuant to the information on the LinkedIn Help page, under "Deceased LinkedIn member – Removing Profile."

Pinterest

After the death of a Pinterest user, a family member can delete this account after providing proof of relationship to the decedent, a link to the Pinterest account, and a copy of the death certificate or obituary.

Google

Google has an option to prepare an inactive-account manager. This tool allows you to decide what will happen with your account if it has been inactive for a pre-determined period of time. After your Google account has been inactive for the designated amount of time, your contacts will receive a message that the account is now inactive. Google also provides you with the option of allowing access to account data, such as your Google drive, email, and YouTube accounts.

Most clients use digital assets every day, but do not have a plan for how they should be managed after incapacity or death. Taking these few steps and having a plan will ensure that these assets are managed properly.

OTHER MATTERS

Genetic Materials

Genetic materials are reproductive materials stored at a facility for future use. If you have genetic materials stored, you will want to decide how you want these items managed, after your passing. Oftentimes, the facility will ask whether these materials should be destroyed after your passing or upon subsequent incapacity. Make sure that you have communicated with the facility about your wishes regarding your genetic materials.

Firearms

In this day and age, firearms is a hot-button topic. If you own firearms, you may want to determine whether a gun trust is appropriate. A gun trust is a specified trust that holds ownership of firearms. This allows the distribution of the firearms after death and will help prevent your named trustee from inadvertently transferring ownership of firearms after death to individuals who are prohibited by federal law from owning firearms.

If you have questions about gun trusts or how to manage the distribution of the guns after death or incapacity, you will want to seek the advice of an estate planning attorney.

CONCLUSION

Estate planning is one of life's details that is often overlooked until it's too late. This area is often ignored because it delves into some of the most intimate and personal details of a person's life, and it difficult to think about. I often have clients come into my office to prepare their estate planning documents after having thought about it for years or even decades.

It is important to not only plan but also review your estate planning documents on a regular basis. I recommend that you review them annually. You should verify that the distribution provisions match your intent, and that you have the correct order for trustees, executors, and agents.

If you do not have any estate planning documents, now is the time to consider preparing them. This is crucial, regardless of your season in life. Following is a checklist for your use.

☑ STEP 2
ESTATE PLANNING CHECKLIST

1. Living Trust

    a. Who are the named trustees and the alternates?

    b. What is the distribution of your assets? Does this distribution reflect your wishes or should it be changed? Review the specific monetary bequests and/or percentages to each of the named beneficiaries. Who are the contingent beneficiaries? Does this reflect your intent? What would happen under different scenarios?

    c. How long ago was the living trust created? Have there been major changes in the law since the creation of the document? Does the document need to be amended and re-stated (a completely new document) or is an amendment (revisions to particular sections) appropriate?

d. Have you moved to another state since the creation of this document? Do you need to revise it to reflect the law of the state where you permanently reside?

e. If you have children or loved ones with special needs, have you created a special-needs trust or arranged for assets to be distributed so that they will not lose their benefits after receiving an inheritance?

f. If you have animals, have your planned for their continuing care? If you have farm animals or exotic animals, does your plan address their unique needs?

2. Last Will and Testament

a. Who is named as your executor? Do you have alternate executors named?

b. Is the distribution of your assets correct?

c. Do you want to leave certain tangible assets to particular individuals? If so, there should be a list and possibly pictures of the items that you wish to distribute.

3. Pour-Over Will (if recognized in your state)

    a. Who are the named executors?

    b. If you have minor children, who is named as named guardian(s) and alternate guardian(s)? Do you wish to keep this the same?

    c. Do you want to leave certain tangible assets to particular individuals? If so, there should be a list and possibly pictures of the items that you wish to distribute.

4. Beneficiary Designations

    a. These are separate from your living trust and your last will and testament. Are these beneficiaries up to date? Have you named a primary beneficiary or beneficiaries and a contingent beneficiary or beneficiaries? Should these be changed? If so, contact the company who administers these accounts and complete the documents needed to change the beneficiaries.

5. Funding the Trust

    a. Are your assets titled in the living trust? Have you reviewed each item and determined which ones need to be titled in the name of the living trust? If assets are not titled in the living trust, you should make arrangements to complete that.

    b. If you own real property, is each piece of real property titled in the name of the living trust?

    c. Are bank accounts and brokerage accounts titled in the name of the living trust?

6. Other Assets

    a. Have you organized your digital assets?

    b. If you have stored genetic materials, have you made a decision regarding what will happen to these materials after you pass away?

    c. Have you create a gun trust or made the proper arrangements for the distribution of your firearms if you become incapacitated or after you die?

7. Financial Power of Attorney

    a. Who is named as your first agent and alternate agents? Is this still correct, or do you want to change these agents?

    b. When was the financial power of attorney created? Is it still up-to-date or does it need to be revised?

    c. Have you moved to another state? You should consider revising your Financial Power of Attorney to reflect the laws of the state where you now reside.

8. Advance Healthcare Directive

    a. Who have you named as your agent and successor agents? Is this still correct?

    b. Do the instructions in your advance healthcare directive still reflect your wishes?

    c. Have you reviewed your organ donation preferences? Does this still reflect your wishes?

d. Have you given a copy of the advance healthcare directive to your primary care physician?

9. Contact Information

   a. Do you have an updated list of all of your contacts? This includes the names, addresses, phone numbers, and email addresses for your beneficiaries, trustees, and agents.

   b. Do you have contact information for all of the individuals you would like contacted if you become incapacitated or after you die?

   c. Do you have contact information for your accountant, lawyers, financial advisors, insurance agents, or any other service providers you use on a consistent basis?

   d. Do you have contact information for your supervisor at work?

   e. Is there a way for your trustee, executor, or agent to access this information after you die or become incapacitated?

Sample Table for Indexing Your Estate Planning Documents

Date Notarized	Title of Document	Creator of Document	Date Modified (what changes were made?)	How are these documents managed (print, cloud, etc.)?
9/30/2017	John and Mary Jones Revocable Living Trust	John and Mary Jones		Copies are located in the home safe and on the cloud-based system.
9/30/2017	Durable Power of Attorney	John and Mary Jones		Copies are located in the home safe and on the cloud-based system.
9/30/2017	Advance Healthcare Directive	John and Mary Jones		Copies are located in the home safe and on the cloud-based system.
9/3/2018	First Amendment to the Revocable Living Trust	John and Mary Jones	Changed trustees	Copies are located in the home safe and on the cloud-based system.

STEP 2 – NOTES AND ACTION ITEMS

- [ ] _____
- [ ] _____
- [ ] _____
- [ ] _____
- [ ] _____
- [ ] _____
- [ ] _____
- [ ] _____
- [ ] _____

STEP 3

Organize Your Financial Information

In Step 2, we discussed your family's roadmap – estate planning. Step 3, financial information and organization, is your family's lifeblood. Organizing your family's financial information will lessen the stress of difficult situations if they already have access to necessary financial information.

This step explores the need to organize your financial information, but does not give specific advice on financial planning. Financial organization is different than financial planning.

I am not making recommendations about the amount of assets needed for retirement, how to invest money, or how much money you should save to plan for the unexpected. This is a personal decision and will depend on many factors, such as your season of life, the number and ages of those individuals in your family, your family's particular needs, and your goals. A holistic financial-planning approach can help you to analyze your unique situation. By planning for different scenarios, you can ensure that your family will have the means to maintain their lifestyle if you become incapacitated or after you pass away. A professional such as a certified financial planner can provide this type of analysis. For more guidance, visit the Let's Make a Plan website at letsmakeaplan.org.

In this book, we are concerned with the why, what, where, and how of organizing your information. Let's begin with the why. In the event that you become incapacitated, your agent will need to know what assets and liabilities you have, so they can continue managing your assets and paying your debts on your behalf. Just having a durable power of attorney will ensure that your agent and successor agents will have the authority to act on your behalf; however, that is not enough. Your agent will need clear, up-to-date information to ensure that proper financial decisions are made on your behalf. Similarly, when you die, you do not want your trustee to struggle without the necessary financial information. This will lead to confusion, which may result in the mismanagement of your assets and debts. The simple act of organizing these documents and information into a system will allow your trusted decision-makers to make appropriate financial decisions.

This step will review each type of asset and debt, and provide guidance on how and where to organize them. Of course, this book may not cover every possible asset and debt. If there are some that are not mentioned, you should create a system for organizing those as well.

Each section is divided into clear sub-sections. We'll begin by reviewing each sub-section and documenting the information that is applicable to you. Let's get started!

DIRT-BASED ASSETS

These are assets such as residences, condominiums, commercial buildings, undeveloped land, and any other type of dirt-based property. In legal parlance, these assets are often referred to as real property, a term used for any property attached to the land. For the purposes of our discussion, I will refer to them as real property.

Buying real property results in the creation of a mountain of documents. After all of the documents are signed and the purchase is completed, many purchasers do not think twice about the documents they signed and merely place them in a file cabinet or box. This section will explore the basic documents related to the purchase of real property and the various ways to organize these documents.

First, let's clarify a few of the terms and the documents. When you purchase real property, there can be over thirty documents for you to review and sign. After the purchase, you will receive additional recoded documents in the mail. These documents can be confusing, as the terms are not always easy to understand. In the following section, I have summarized the main documents you should consider reviewing and organizing.

Grant Deed / Warranty Deed / Special Warranty Deed

Depending on the state in which you purchased the real property, this document may be called a grant deed, warranty deed, special warranty deed, or something else. This is the document that shows title for the real property. In other words, this document proves legal ownership of the real property. It contains information regarding the seller (grantor), the buyer (grantee), the purchase date, how the title was taken, and the date the transaction was completed. The document is recorded with the county recorder's office in the county where the property is located. Some of the basic information in this document are summarized as follows:

Ownership information: On the document, it will refer to the grantor (seller) and grantee (buyer). This section of the document states the parties to the transaction. It will also state whether the property was sold/purchased by a married couple, married but purchasing separately, or a single person. There may also be information stating whether title is held as joint tenants or tenancy in common. Each delineation has ramifications. If you are unsure how this affects your property, you will want to consult with a qualified professional.

Contact information: The top half of the deed will list the name and address of the owner. Underneath this information there may be a unique identification number. In many counties, property identification numbers are assigned to each particular piece of real property. This will appear on your deed and property tax bill and is sometimes referred to as an assessor's parcel number. In other counties it may be referred to by a different term, and some may not use a parcel number at all. This varies depending on the county where the property is located.

In every grant deed, there will be a legal description, which contains the measurements made by the surveyor. A legal description may be a lot and block description, which applies to properties located in subdivisions, or it may be a metes and bounds description, which applies to non-division property. Some properties may combine elements of both.

Oftentimes, the legal description will be attached to the deed and referred to as Exhibit A, or it may appear within the body of the document. It is easy to spot the legal description, as it will have specific surveying information. The important thing to remember is that a legal description is required in any recorded documents conveying title.

Now let's differentiate the grant deed from other documents related to real property.

The Deed of Trust

The deed of trust shows that the title of your home is held by a trustee as security for the repayment of a loan. It is easy to confuse a deed of trust with a grant deed, and clients often mix these two up. The grant deed shows the title or ownership of your home, while the deed of trust contains the terms of your mortgage.

In the deed of trust, you will see terms such as trustor, beneficiary, and trustee. The trustor is the borrower or debtor; the beneficiary is the lender/creditor; and the trustee holds the legal title. There may be multiple deed of trust documents associated with each piece of real property you own. Each time you refinance, a new deed of trust is created because you have entered into a new mortgage. Each subsequent deed of trust is recorded with the county recorder where the real property is located.

Quit-Claim Deed

A quit-claim deed is a document that relinquishes ownership of the property to another individual or individuals. The quit-claim only conveys as much of the property that the grantor is able to convey; in other words, you cannot quit-claim more of an interest than you own.

Interspousal Transfer Deed

An interspousal transfer deed is a deed that transfers property interest between spouses. Typically this document is recorded as a result of an addition of a spouse to the real property or as part of a divorce settlement.

Deed of Reconveyance

The deed of reconveyance, or satisfaction of the deed of trust, documents that the loan/mortgage has been paid off and the borrower is no longer responsible for making mortgage payments.

These are some of the basic documents that may be associated with a parcel of land. This is not meant to be an exhaustive list; your real property may also have other documents recorded that are not mentioned here. If you have questions about the significance of a particular document, you may want to obtain professional advice.

Chain of Title

The chain of title refers to all documents that have been recorded with respect to a particular parcel of land. At the recorder's office in the county where the property is located, you can search the documents related to a particular parcel of land and track ownership changes.

The documents will be arranged chronologically, so you can review all of the documents recorded with respect to the parcel of land.

Homeowner's Insurance

Homeowner's insurance covers damage to the interior or exterior of your home. Choosing the amount of coverage you need will depend on your unique situation. You may also opt for additional coverage for earthquakes and floods, depending on the location of the real property. It is advisable to speak to a reputable insurance agent.

Next, you should assess whether you need to schedule any personal items on your homeowner's insurance policy. Scheduling an asset on your policy means that a particular item is covered by your insurance policy in the event of theft or loss. For example, jewelry, coin collections, and paintings are some of the most commonly scheduled items. These high-value items are scheduled because the homeowner's policy only allows a fixed amount of coverage if the item is lost or stolen. If you need to schedule a particular item on your policy, you'll have to contact your insurance agent. You will need to obtain an appraisal of the item, and pay an additional fee for coverage of these items. Finally, if you have a living trust, you may also want to add the trust as an additional insured on the homeowner's policy.

I recommend creating a separate file for the homeowner's insurance policy documents for each of your parcels of real property. This file should be placed near the ownership files for each parcel of property.

Title Insurance

Title insurance protects your home from chain of title disputes, cloud on title actions, or property line disputes. Your title insurance is designed to protect against these disputes. Title insurance is part of the purchase of the property and covers you while you own the property. Subsequent title insurance policies may be issued when your home is refinanced, but this policy is for the benefit of the mortgage company.

A copy of the title insurance will be in the original sales file. If you need to review this policy in the future, you can find it in the property file.

Umbrella Policy

An umbrella policy is an additional liability policy that protects you from lawsuits. It provides additional coverage on top of your homeowner's insurance and/or vehicle insurance. If you have this type of coverage, you should keep a copy of the policy in your insurance folder.

Documents Needed for Each Piece of Real Property

Separate folders should be created for each piece of real property. There should be a folder for the original purchase documents, all refinance documents, copies of the homeowner's insurance, property tax information, lease agreements, and maintenance records and receipts.

Having separate files for each type of document will make it much easier to find items in the future. For example, under repairs and maintenance, you may want to create separate folders for electrical repairs, plumbing repairs, roofing, landscaping, and so forth. In each of these folders, keep copies of the invoices, receipts, and warranty information.

Homeowners – How to Manage Real Property Documents

It's easy to become overwhelmed by the sheer number of documents associated with real property ownership. An easy way to organize these documents is by utilizing a folder file system. The first folder contains your original purchase documents – the contract and all of the additional documents. The second file contains the recorded documents. I suggest that whenever a document is mailed to you from the county recorder, you place the document in this file in chronological order.

Of course, you should prepare this filing system for each property you own. This way you have a complete file for all of the documents recorded for each property. For easy reference, place tabs on documents such as the grant deed or deed of reconveyance.

There is a public recordkeeping system for real properties. In each county where the real property is located, there is a public office in charge of cataloging these documents. To locate the office, search "land records" or "real property records" plus the name of the county and state where the property is located.

Real property records are public records. Depending on the county, the office where they're kept may be called the recorder's office or clerk's office, or they may be managed by the local courthouse. If you want copies of any of the recorded documents, you can go to the designated office and request them. You can also mail a letter requesting copies of the documents you want. In some counties, you can order these documents online. There is a cost for copies, which varies by county.

Timeshares

I recommend creating a folder for each of your timeshares. Each folder should contain the contract, the deed, or the certificates of ownership. You should also place the monthly statements in the folder.

Renters

If you are renting an apartment or home, you should have a folder containing a current copy of your lease and all amendments, a copy of your current renter's insurance policies, and any other relevant documents.

PERSONAL PROPERTY, HOUSEHOLD FURNISHINGS, AND BUSINESS PROPERTY

When it comes to personal property and business property, it is useful to remember the three I's: have an Inventory, organize this Information, and maintain a proper level of Insurance.

Inventory

Taking the time to organize a list of your household furnishings, personal property, and business property is an important part of your overall organizational process.

The first step is to complete an inventory of all of this property. Following is a table you can use. It is advisable to include as much of this information as possible.

Description of item	Date obtained	Amount paid	Serial number, if applicable	Other distinguishing characteristics or additional information

After you have completed this table, you may want to create a physical file and include any manuals, receipts, or appraisals that you have and include a copy of the inventory list in the file. You may also want to take a video of the items and/or take pictures of the items.

After preparing this inventory, you should consider storing the list, video, and photographs on the cloud, or, at a minimum, emailing it to yourself or other family members so it can be easily retrieved. If there is a natural disaster or some other type of calamity, this information can be invaluable. As part of this process, you should decide multiple ways in which you can access this information and who will have access to it.

Insurance

The last step is determining whether you have adequate insurance for these items. Your insurance agent can help you review your insurance limits and provide guidance on whether you have adequate insurance.

ORGANIZATION OF OTHER FINANCIAL ASSETS AND LIABILITIES

A current, up-to-date list of assets and liabilities is integral to the eight-step plan. I cannot stress enough how important it is to keep an updated list of all of your assets. This will be crucial if you become incapacitated and after death. This information is necessary for your named agent and successor trustee.

This list should be created and updated on a yearly basis. One easy way to remember to keep your list up to date is to mark your calendar each year with the date of review. You may decide to do this at the beginning of each year or when you are preparing your taxes.

Some of the assets you will want to organize are as follows:

- Bank accounts – checking and savings
- Certificates of deposit/mutual funds/brokerage accounts
- US savings bonds
- Retirement accounts
- IRA
- 401(k)
- Annuities

- Life insurance

For each of these assets, you will want to keep a file folder. If you only receive electronic statements, it is a good idea to print them quarterly and place them in the appropriate file folder.

Intellectual Property

Do you have patents, have copyrights, or receive royalties? It is advisable to create a list of these assets, and make this list available to your family so they can continue any benefits they may be entitled to.

Credit Cards

For each credit card or department-store card, you may want to keep a table containing the relevant information so it can easily be managed and tracked. The information you may want to document is found in the following table.

Credit card company and their contact information	Card type and card number	Balance	Credit limit	Date payment due	Electronic payment – date, amount, and which bank account

Credit Reports

If you print out your credit reports on a regular basis, you should place them in a designated folder. This is a good way to compare how your credit score has changed over time and ascertain whether your score is sufficient to reach your financial goals.

Social Security Reports

If you print these out or receive these in the mail, you will want to keep a file for these reports.

Other Assets (Bank Accounts, CDs, IRAs, 401(k)s, Annuities, Brokerage Accounts, Stocks)

For assets such as bank accounts, certificates of deposit, IRA accounts, 401(k) accounts, annuities, brokerage accounts, and stocks, it is advisable to prepare tables with the pertinent information. Following is a table for your use. You may want to include additional information as well.

Name of institution and contact information	Type of account	Name on account and account number or last 4 digits	Approximate value	Is there a beneficiary named? Have you named a primary and secondary beneficiaries? If yes, is this up-to-date?	Is the asset titled in the living trust?

US Savings Bonds

You will want to keep a detailed list of each of your US savings bonds. Following is a sample table for your use.

Type of bonds, which series	Number	Savings bond number	How is it titled?	Maturity date

Life Insurance

For each life insurance policy, you will want to keep a table including the contact information of the insurance company, the type of life insurance, the face value amount, and the names of the beneficiaries. As discussed earlier, you may want to name primary and contingent beneficiaries. These beneficiaries should be updated to match your intent.

Name of insurance company, contact information, and name of insured	Type of life insurance – term or universal?	Face or cash value amount	Named beneficiaries – primary and contingent

Income Tax Returns

A separate file should be kept for each year's federal and state tax returns. You will want to keep them for the appropriate number of years. These tax returns are particularly helpful for the trustee and will be used by the trustee to prepare the trust tax return after death.

Safe-Deposit Box

A folder should be created for each of your safe-deposit boxes. Be sure to include the contract. It is important to verify that all of the identifying information is included – for example, the branch, safe-deposit box number, and names of the signors on the box. In the folder, you may want to keep the key to the box in a clearly marked envelope.

This is a good time to review the designated signors on the account. Each person who is a designated signor can access the box at any time with the box number, key, and proof of identity. If you feel uncomfortable with other individuals having immediate access, you may want to revise the signor list.

If you are the only signor on the safe-deposit box, your trustee/executor can gain access to the box if they have a death certificate and a valid and properly executed living trust or will. They would take these items into the bank along with the key — if they don't have a key a duplicate can be made, but there will be an additional cost.

Oftentimes, clients will tell me that they know the decedent had a safe-deposit box, but they have no idea which bank or branch. This can be easily avoided by using documentation.

Vehicles

Create a folder for each of your vehicles with sub-sections or sub-folders for different types of documents. The first sub-folder will contain the ownership information, pink slip, and registration information. The second will include the warranty information and maintenance records. It is important to track information about your car warranties. You should review the warranty coverage, the date of expiration, and the terms, such as the number of years it's valid and whether it expires after the car has reached a certain number of miles.

An additional section should include a copy of your car insurance policy. You will also want to place proof of car insurance in your glove box and in your wallet, and keep a copy of your vehicle registration in your glove box as well.

Another section of the folder should include information pertaining to maintenance. This is the place to keep all of your repair receipts and invoices. It makes it easier if you organize it by year. On the front of the service records you may want to prepare a table specifying the date of repair, what was repaired, and the cost. This makes it easy for you to review service records in the future.

I keep a separate folder for the oil-change records. You may want to include a table with the date of the oil change, mileage at the time of the change, and any notes. Behind this table, place all of the oil-change invoices. This is particularly important if you have a warranty for your car. Many warranties will be voided if you don't change the oil at the recommended intervals.

If you are involved in a car accident, I recommend keeping a separate section for the accident reports, police reports, correspondence from the insurance company, service records, and any warranties pertaining to the repair.

I'm often asked whether vehicles need to be re-titled into the name of the living trust. Typically you won't need to unless it is over the probate limit for your state. However, the specific requirement will depend on the state you live in, the value of your vehicle, and the probate limits.

Boats, Planes, and Recreational Vehicles

If you own a boat, plane, or recreational vehicle, you will want to keep a separate organizational folder for each. This folder should contain the maintenance records, registration information, and insurance information. Depending on the number of documents, you may want to create sub-folders for each of these items. If you have a living trust, you may want to re-title your airplane into the name of the living trust. There are specific documents that must be completed and submitted to the Federal Aviation Agency.

If you own a boat, you may also want to re-title the boat into the name of the living trust. Again, there are specific requirements that need to be followed before you can complete this process.

Promissory Notes and Personal Loans

For each promissory note, you should include a copy of this document in a folder containing this document. If the promissory note was recorded, include a copy of this document in your folder and add this information to your list of assets. You should also keep a document containing all of the payments that have been made.

Judgments

Keep copies of any judgments you have against an individual or corporation. If the judgment was paid, include a copy of the satisfaction of judgment. If it has not been paid in full and the individual is making payments, keep a list of payments paid and those that are still owed. On the other hand, if there is a judgment against you, then keep records related to the payments made.

Health Insurance

A separate folder should be created for your health insurance information. This folder should include a current copy of your health insurance policy and a copy of your health insurance card. Plan summaries and documents pertaining to health insurance payments should also be included in this folder.

Disability Insurance and Long-Term-Care Insurance

A separate folder should be created for your disability insurance and long-term-care policies. In these folders, include copies of your policies, correspondence, and any other relevant information.

Your List of Advisors

For each of your professional advisors, prepare a current list with their name and contact information. This list should include all attorneys, certified financial planners, insurance agents, certified public accountant, and so forth. In this list, you will also want to include notes or information that could be useful for your trustee or agent.

Debts

For each debt, it is important to keep an up-to-date list or table containing pertinent information for each debt. In the following pages, there is a list of various types of debts organized by the type of debt. Each of the categories has a list of details you should include. Of course, depending on your particular situation, there may be other debts not included in this list; this is merely a template you can use to create your own.

Financial Obligations

Mortgage

First Mortgage
- Name and contact information of the institution
- Loan number
- Amount of loan
- Interest rate
- Type of loan
- Length of loan
- Loan documents and deed of trust

Second Mortgage/HELOC
- Name and contact information of the institution
- Loan number
- Amount of loan
- Interest rate
- Type of loan
- Length of loan

Vehicle Loans
- Name of the institution
- Amount of loan
- Length of loan
- Date of pay-off

Other Loans

Credit Cards
- Card number
- Contact information of the company
- Credit card limit
- Credit card balance

Utilities
- Electricity, gas, water, garbage
- Phone, internet, and cable provider

Student Loans
- Company name
- Type of loan
- Account number
- Amount and interest rate

Tax Payments
- Estimated quarterly payments
- For any outstanding tax obligations, the amount, type, and payment plan

Child Support or Spousal Support Obligations
- County collecting the child support or spousal support obligations
- Monthly payment amount

Automatic Deposits and Payments

In this day and age, more people are utilizing online payment options. This is convenient but can cause a whole host of problems if this information is not organized. Some of these automatic payments may be large debts, such as a mortgage, or smaller debts, such as utility bills and credit card payments.

The management of these automatic deposits and payments becomes complicated after someone passes away or is incapacitated. I often meet with clients who think that their loved one had automatic deposits or payments set up, but do not have any information regarding the specifics.

As part of the organization of your family records, I recommend that you create a list of all automatic deposits and payments. When you make changes or add something new, remember to update your list. I have included a table below to help you organize this information.

Creditor's Name Depositor's Name	Contact Information	User Name	Password	Date of Deposit or Payment	Amount of Deposit or Payment	Account (from which it is withdrawn or deposited)

Business Owners

For business owners, it is especially important to keep well-organized financial records. In the following pages, there is a checklist that will help you to organize this information. This is a general list, but should be tailored to meet the needs of your particular business.

If you have business partners, you should schedule a meeting to organize the documents and keep them in a mutually agreed-upon place. You may also wish to digitize these records and ensure that the other partners have access to them when needed. If you are a sole practitioner, you will want to gather all of the necessary information and ensure that your agent for the financial power of attorney and successor trustee know how to access it.

Some of the items you'll want to gather are as follows:

Legal Documents
- If you have rented an office or retail space, you should have a file with the lease and contact information for your landlord.
- If you have created an LLC, S-Corp, C-Corp, or partnership, you should have a copy of the initial filing documents and all subsequent filings.
- If you own commercial properties, you should have copies of all of the deeds as well as the rental agreements for the tenants.

Insurance
- Copies of all of your insurance policies, including malpractice insurance and general liability policies

Operating Information
- Access information, such as a list of where the keys are located for the office space or retail space, and the access code for the alarm system
- A copy of your business permit

Contact Information
- Names and contact information for all of your employees
- Names and contact information for your accountant/bookkeeper, attorney, and insurance agent
- Information on suppliers and vendors that are regularly used

Taxes
- Filed tax returns for the business

Financial Information
- Business bank accounts, including the names, contact information, and account numbers
- Information about the business credit cards and promissory notes

Expenses
- A list of the utilities for the business, including payments for electricity, water, and internet
- A list of all of the expenses for the business

Digital Assets
- A list of all URLs and websites for the business, including expiration dates for URLs and access information for websites
- A list of the websites regularly used for your business, including the log-in information and passwords
- All of the social media sites that are used for the business, including all of the usernames and passwords

Continuing Education
- All information on subscriptions and memberships
- All information on professional licenses and continuing education

Intellectual Property
- Information on any business trademarks, copyrights, or patents your business has attained

Other
- Create an inventory of all of your business assets. This should include descriptions of the items, dates purchased, amounts paid for them, and serial numbers.

- Include information regarding any storage units, with information on how to access them if needed.
- Review your estate planning documents and ensure that there is a sub-section that allows the trustee to continue the business or close the business if you become incapacitated or pass away.
- Include a copy of your business succession plan.

Of course, this is not an all-inclusive checklist. Depending on the type and size of your business, you may need additional information and documents. Taking the time to gather this information and creating a plan for the organization of these documents will decrease the possibility of a business disruption when something unexpected occurs.

CONCLUSION

Congratulations on reviewing your financial documents and organizing them. Let's move on to the next step, which is the organization of your current healthcare information!

☑ STEP 3
FINANCIAL INFORMATION CHECKLIST

1. Assets

    a. Real Property

        i. Do you have a copy of the most recent grant deed or warranty deed?

        ii. Do you have copies of your mortgage documents?

        iii. Do you have your homeowner's insurance information?

        iv. Have you organized your maintenance records?

    b. Rental Property

        i. Do you have copies of your lease agreement?

        ii. Do you have a copy of your renter's insurance?

c. Personal Property

   i. Remember the three I's

      A. Inventory: Make an inventory of all of your personal property. This may include a written list as well as a video record.

      B. Information

      C. Insurance

d. Financial Assets

   i. Create a list of all of your bank accounts, CD's brokerage accounts, US Savings Bonds, IRA's, 401(k)s, annuities, and life insurance. For each of these assets, prepare a list with the name and contact information of the institution, account identification, named primary and contingent beneficiaries, and any other pertinent information.

e. Safe-deposit box information

f. Information on your vehicles

   i. Title and loan information

  ii. Maintenance information, including an oil-change log

 g. Information on boats and planes

2. Debts

 a. Make a list of all debts, including credit cards, loans, promissory notes, and student loans.

3. Insurance

 a. Health insurance

 b. Disability insurance

 c. Long-term-care insurance

4. A list of automatic deposits and payments

5. Business owners – please refer to the checklist in this chapter

STEP 3 – NOTES AND ACTION ITEMS

☐ _____

☐ _____

☐ _____

☐ _____

☐ _____

☐ _____

☐ _____

☐ _____

☐ _____

STEP 4

Organize Your Current Healthcare Information

Now we are going to switch gears from financial information to healthcare information. Current healthcare information is an integral life detail. It is important to organize it and track it as it changes and evolves. Having this documentation readily available will ensure that you have the medical information you need when you see a new doctor or healthcare provider.

Additionally, it is important to have this information organized and available in case there's an emergency. If you (or a loved one) have an accident or a medical event, the doctors will immediately need to know the medical history, such as prescription medications, allergies, and past surgical procedures.

Primary Care Physician

I recommend maintaining a separate file for your primary care physician. Keep information such as the following:

- Copies of blood tests in chronological order. This way you can easily track and compare blood test results. You may want to use tabs to help you locate them in the future.
- Documentation regarding weight and blood pressure.

- Copies of any test results and the treatment plans, in chronological order.
- The questions that were prepared prior to your appointment with the doctor and his or her responses.
- Any other documents or information your doctor gives you.
- Medical insurance claims and processed claim information.

This is a good time to verify that your primary care doctor has the most recent copy of your advance healthcare directive or living will, which will be discussed in depth in **Step 5**.

Specialists

I recommend keeping a separate file for each of your specialists. These may include cardiologists, internal medicine doctors, ophthalmologists, dermatologists, and so forth.

For each of these specialists, you should keep the same information you keep for your primary care physician. Your notes, test results, and any other documentation should be placed in this file. Organizing by doctor and maintaining separate files will make it much easier to locate information in the future.

If you have a chronic condition, this could be a good time to request a complete copy of your medical records. This may include copies of X-rays, test results, and reports. HIPAA (the Health Insurance Portability and Accountability Act of 1996) is federal legislation that requires your doctors to keep your data private. Its other purpose is to allow you to request copies of your healthcare records. HIPAA requires your doctor to provide your records, in either electronic or physical form, when you properly request them.

These records should be organized so you can track your condition and also easily share information with other doctors, when the need arises.

Optometrist

For your optometrist, keep a copy of any notes from your appointments as well as your eyeglass and contact-lens prescriptions.

Dentist

For your dentist, keep notes for the dentist, dental insurance claim forms, claim payments, and receipts. If you have had more extensive dental procedures, you may want to keep separate files with the information and records.

Yearly Tests, Screenings, and Vaccinations

It is a good idea to organize your yearly tests, screenings, and vaccinations for each family member. For each family member, keep a list with the date of vaccination, types of screenings, tests, and any other relevant information. Keep copies of these tests and screenings in your file for easy reference.

Prescriptions

Having an up-to-date list of prescriptions is crucial. You should keep a current list of your medications, their dosages, the doctor who prescribed them, the date prescribed, and any other pertinent information. This information should be updated when changes are made to your medications. The updated list should be kept in your medical file. Following is a sample table.

Name:_____

Date Prescribed	Medication and the purpose of the medication	Dosage information (strength and the number of times you take it each day)	Prescribing doctor	Notes

This table should be updated on a regular basis. Along with this table, I suggest you also keep a copy of the information provided by the pharmacy describing the purpose of the medication, medication instructions, and possible side effects.

You should also consider how this information will be accessed in the event of an emergency situation. In these types of situations, you may be unable to think clearly or remember the names of your prescription drugs, so it's a good idea to keep a card in your wallet with all of your up-to-date prescription drug information.

You should also consider keeping this list in your phone or tablet, glove box, or day planner. Having easy access to this information will decrease your stress level. This is particularly important because most people can remember the names of their prescriptions, but may not remember the dosage amounts.

Assistive Devices

If you use assistive devices, such as an hearing aid, electric wheelchair, or a CPAP machine, it is advisable to have a file for each of these items. In that file, you should include the doctor's order, copies of warranties, user instructions, and the serial number or any other type of identifying information for each of these items.

Your Medical History and Family History of Illness

Whenever you go to a new doctor, the patient questionnaire always includes questions about your medical history and for your family. As part of Step 4, it is helpful to prepare a list of this information and update it on a regular basis.

For your personal medical history, prepare a current list of prescriptions, surgeries, tests, and procedures. This should be listed chronologically and kept in your personal medical history file.

For your family medical history, you may want to acquire the following information for your parents, grandparents, and siblings:

- Chronic conditions: For each chronic condition, document the type of condition they have or had, the medications prescribed, and the length of time they had or have had this condition. For cancer-related diseases, you will also want to document your history of cancer in your family. This would include the name of the family member who has cancer, the type of cancer, when it was diagnosed, and how it was treated.
- Surgeries: The type of surgeries they had and the dates of the surgeries, if known.

- If deceased, when did they pass away? What was the cause of death and the date of death?
- Any other pertinent information regarding your family health history and/or documents.

This list should be updated as new information is acquired.

List of Allergies

A current list of allergies for each family member can be important for future reference and treatment, particularly those related to medications, bee stings, food, latex, and so forth, especially in an emergency.

How and Where to Organize Medical Records

How and where you choose to organize this information will depend on your personal preferences. You might organize these documents in paper form, digital form, or both. There may be other medical information not reviewed in this chapter that you will also want to include.

Having this information organized and readily available will make a tremendous difference during times of stress, such as a medical emergency. I suggest keeping information such as prescriptions and doctors' names on a card in your wallet, or perhaps as a list on your cell phone or tablet, depending on what you regularly have with you.

It will also help you and your family when you make an appointment with a healthcare provider and they need medical history information.

In our next step, we will explore a similar topic – future healthcare. Let's get started!

☑ STEP 4
CURRENT HEALTHCARE CHECKLIST

1. Documents and notes concerning appointments with your primary care physician

2. Documents and notes concerning appointments with specialists

3. Optometrist information

4. Dental information

5. A list of all tests, screenings, and vaccinations for each family member

6. A list of your current prescription medications, including a physical copy, a digital copy, and a small laminated card in your purse or wallet

7. A list of any assistive devices you use, including serial numbers and warranty information

8. Information regarding your personal medical family history

9. A list of allergies for each family member and the medications that are taken for these allergies

10. A plan for how and where to organize these documents and information

STEP 4 – NOTES AND ACTION ITEMS

☐ _____

☐ _____

☐ _____

☐ _____

☐ _____

☐ _____

☐ _____

☐ _____

☐ _____

STEP 5

Document Your Future Healthcare Decisions

An advance healthcare directive, which in many states is referred to as a living will, is a document that everyone, regardless of their season of life, should complete. This document directs your agent to make healthcare decisions for you if you are incapacitated. It is so important, in fact, that Congress has declared April 16th of each year National Healthcare Directives Day.

There are many resources online that can help you create this document. To find one of the many non-profit organizations and hospitals that can guide you through the process, simply do an online search for "advance healthcare directive" or "living will" along with your state, and you will find a variety of resources.

FUTURE HEALTHCARE

Beyond "Pull the Plug"

As an estate planning attorney, I have heard certain phrases hundreds of times. The phrase "just pull the plug – I do not want to be a burden" is one of them.

There must be a better way to describe end-of-life decisions than just saying "pull the plug."

What does this mean? How did this phrase even get into our vernacular? First of all, there is no plug that is pulled. The machines are turned off and the IVs are taken out.

Regardless of the details, the phrase "pulling the plug" does not describe at which point you would like to stop receiving aggressive health treatment, and does not provide any useful information. It assumes that your named agent will know what to do at the appropriate time. It puts a lot of pressure on your agent to make such an important decision based on vague instructions.

We all have certain ideas when it comes to the management of our future healthcare. As we pass through our life seasons, we continue to develop our healthcare wishes and have an idea of what we would want under certain circumstances. While most individuals have specific desires for future healthcare, only a small fraction of individuals have talked to their loved ones regarding this subject, and even fewer have created a healthcare directive.

Creating a medical directive can be challenging, but having this document in place will greatly decrease the amount of stress on your loved ones because they will not have to speculate or guess regarding your preferred medical treatment.

First, we'll begin with some basic medical terminology.

The Challenge of Making Treatment Decisions

Admittedly, asking a client to make medical decisions about a medical event that has not happened and may never happen is a challenging conversation.

Most individuals do not have any context for this situation except for what they've seen in the movies, watched on the news, or heard in stories from friends and acquaintances. I believe that is why clients commonly refer to end-of-life decisions as "pulling the plug." Without proper context and information, it's no wonder most people have not prepared a medical directive.

The first section of a medical directive will state your end-of-life decisions. This is information about the type of medical treatment you would want under particular circumstances. In the following sections, the common medical terms are reviewed. Of course, this is merely an overview. This is a topic you may want to discuss further with your estate planning attorney or your medical provider.

Common Medical Treatments

One of the most common medical responses is CPR, or cardiopulmonary resuscitation. CPR is where chest compressions are applied approximately 100 times per minute. CPR may be effective, but it depends on your health at the time of the administration of this procedure. For someone who does not have a serious illness, there is a strong chance that the heart can be restarted. However, if someone has a chronic health condition or is an advanced age, this technique may not be successful. In these cases, CPR could cause additional damage and the person may not recover. If you decide that you would not want CPR or would want CPR only under certain circumstances, you can include these directions in your medical directive. These are often referred to as a Do Not Resuscitate Order, or DNR. If you have a DNR and your heart stops beating and you are not breathing, medical personnel will not administer CPR.

A ventilator is used if you are unable to breath on your own. The ventilator has a tube that is placed through the mouth and down the trachea to pump air into the lungs.

A ventilator or life support may be necessary for a short period of time, but depending on the health of the individual it may be necessary for months or even years. That is why it is important for individuals to decide how long they would want to be on this type of life support and under what circumstances.

When making decisions about this issue, it is important for you to think about your own health condition and values. Some people don't want to remain on life support indefinitely if there is no chance of recovery. Others want to remain on life support for as long as possible, in the hopes that they will recover. This is where a properly crafted medical directive can help your family –they will have guidance from you if you are in a situation where you can't communicate.

For example, when my dad was on life support, our family had no guidance. When my parents created their estate plan, the attorney placed two blank advance healthcare forms in their binder with a sticky note asking them to complete them. When my dad was placed on life support, medical personnel asked us whether there was an advance healthcare directive. When we reviewed the binder and looked under that tab, we were dismayed to find that the form was blank.

My father was on life support for a month while my mom tried to figure out what to do. My dad never discussed this issue with my mom or any of his kids. We were at a loss and did not know what to do. He remained unconscious during this time and we felt stressed, guilty, and confused because we were lost. We all speculated about what he would want, but making life-and-death decisions based on assumptions or feelings is the wrong way to handle these difficult situations. I became an estate planning attorney as a result of this, because I don't want families to go through what we went through.

Unfortunately, this situation is all too common. I urge you to take all necessary actions now and prepare and execute this document.

Pain relief refers to treatments used to ease pain during an illness. Depending on the situation, pain relief could include treatments such as morphine to help keep a patient calm and pain-free. If pain relief is administered, it may hasten your death. In other words, you may die sooner as a result of the medication. Depending on your view regarding the use of pain-relief treatment, you may want to specify under what circumstances you would want it.

Another type of medical treatment is hydration and nutrition. This is where an IV or tube is used to provide sustenance. Depending on your views, you may want to address this topic in your medical directive. Some individuals only want this treatment for a specific period of time and under certain circumstances. In your medical directive, you should address this issue and give your agent guidance on want you would want under various circumstances.

When considering these different options and completing the advance healthcare directive, it's a good idea to review these matters with your estate planning attorney or a medical professional.

These are difficult decisions, but with planning and research, you can determine the type of medical treatment you would or would not want under particular circumstances. For many, it's about age. Some clients want more aggressive treatment at earlier ages and less aggressive treatment at later ages, if they have chronic health conditions. Many clients have specific ideas regarding what constitutes good quality of life and poor quality of life and prepare a medical directive that documents these beliefs. Others have particular religious or spiritual beliefs that their end-of-life decisions need to align with.

If you don't know where to start, there are many publications and organizations that can provide information to help guide you through the process. In my practice, I have found that Go Wish cards, a game that encourages people to talk about their end-of-life wishes, can help clients. An internet search will provide a lot of resources.

Naming an Agent or Surrogate

Along with your end-of-life wishes, you will also need to name an agent or surrogate to make arrangements for your chosen course of medical treatment. The agent starts to make these decisions if a medical professional determines that you are physically or mentally incapacitated.

The choice of agent is a crucial decision. Your primary or first agent should be someone who is able to make decisions under stressful conditions, is comfortable communicating information to family and friends, and has the ability to effectively communicate with medical personnel and follow your specific instructions.

The role of a healthcare agent is a stressful position. This person is often the point person between the medical provider and the family and friends. This should be a person who knows you well and will have the emotional strength to follow your wishes, even if the course of action is opposed by family members. This person will be your advocate when you are unable to speak for yourself. The agent will manage your treatment and ask the necessary questions to ensure that your wishes are honored. Of course, before you name an agent, you need to discuss this document and role with them and make sure they agree to serving in this capacity.

I recommend that you name a first agent and alternates. It is always a good idea to have alternate agents in the event that the primary agent is unavailable or unable to act on your behalf. While it is tempting to name co-agents, this arrangement can lead to problems if they are unable to coordinate their actions, work together, or agree. As discussed in Step 2, I recommend naming a primary agent and one or two alternates.

Your document should also include a HIPAA release, which will allow your agents to discuss your health situation with your doctors and obtain copies of your medical records.

Organ Donation

Your advance healthcare directive or living will should also include your instructions regarding organ donation.

One of the most shocking calls I have ever received was from the organ-donation center the morning after my sister's death. We were at a loss for how to respond, because my sister had never talked about death, let alone organ donation. Our family ultimately decided to authorize organ donation because my sister was such a giving, generous, and loving person. But we made this decision based on speculation. We did not have much time to make a decision because time was of the essence.

If you have never been through this process, it is daunting. I spent the next hour and a half answering all sorts of questions. They had reviewed her medical records, but they wanted to know about her personal habits and information not contained in the records. I answered as best I could, but I barely made it through the process. At one point I wanted to stop, but I kept answering the questions because it was my feeling that my sister would have wanted to donate her organs. Many years have passed, but that decision still haunts me. I have agonized over it because her wishes were not documented. I will never know whether we followed her wishes.

I hope that you and your loved ones will not have to make a decision of this magnitude based on speculation. Taking the time to decide this issue and documenting your choices will save your family heartache and worry.

When I discuss this question with clients, they find it very difficult to answer if they have not already thought about organ donation.

Many of my clients have preconceived notions about organ donations. Many believe they are too old to donate organs. However, depending on the health of the decedent, it is often possible to donate organs at an advanced age.

When clients think of organ donation, they typically assume it refers to heart, kidney, lung, or liver transplants; however, there is also a need for cartilage, tissue, skin, and corneas. Before the transplant is approved, the medical records of the donor will be reviewed and the organs will be tested for HIV, cancer cells, and infection.

Regardless of age, if the organs are viable they can be donated.

You can decide to donate these organs for transplant or for other purposes, such as research or education. There are various options, including the possibility of donating your entire body to a medical school. These willed-body programs will be discussed in the next step.

Once you have made this decision and documented it on your advance healthcare directive, you should find out if there is an organ-donor registry in your state. If there is, you may want to consider registering.

How and Where to Organize and Manage Your Advance Healthcare Directive or Living Will

Once your medical directive has been completed, you should give a copy to your primary care physician, who will put this document in your medical file.

Additionally, keep the original advance healthcare directive with the rest of your estate planning documents. You should let your agent know where this document is located or provide them with a paper or electronic copy. You may also want to keep a copy in a digital repository system. I also keep a copy of this document on my phone and tablet; it's helpful to have a downloaded copy on your phone, since most people have their phones with them at all times.

In your wallet, you may want to keep a card with the names and phone numbers of your agents and alternate agents. In the event that you are unconscious, medical personnel will know whom to contact. When you travel, you should take a copy of this document with you, either a physical copy or one downloaded to your phone or tablet. I also suggest that you keep one in the glove box of your car. Keeping multiple copies in various places means it's readily available in an emergency.

As discussed earlier, many states have a registry system for advance healthcare directives or living wills. If your state does, it's a good idea to register it with that agency.

Now that you have completed your advance-care planning and have created a system for managing it, we will move on to your final wishes.

☑ STEP 5
FUTURE MEDICAL CARE CHECKLIST

1. Create a properly executed advance healthcare directive or living will document that includes the nomination of a surrogate decision-maker and alternates, instructions concerning end-of-life decisions, and instructions regarding organ donation.

2. After your advance healthcare directive or living will is executed, give a copy of this document to your primary care physician or specialist to place in your medical record.

3. Keep an electronic copy in a digital repository system and on your phone or tablet.

4. Create an emergency contact card to carry in your wallet that includes the names and numbers of your medical decision-makers.

5. If your state has a registry system, you may want to consider forwarding a copy of the advance healthcare directive to this agency.

STEP 5 – NOTES AND ACTION ITEMS

☐ _____

☐ _____

☐ _____

☐ _____

☐ _____

☐ _____

☐ _____

☐ _____

☐ _____

STEP 6

Prepare and Plan for Your Final Wishes

Out of all of the eight steps, this subject tends to be the most difficult. When I mention the words "burial" or "cremation," I can see the fear in my clients' eyes. It is typically the last thing they want to discuss. However, having this decision made beforehand will save your loved ones a lot of trauma. If you die unexpectedly without expressing your wishes, your family and loved ones will be forced to make these decisions without knowing what you wanted.

Personally, this has happened to me three times. These were the three most horrible meetings I have ever attended. We were forced to make decisions based on what "he or she would have wanted." I remember we said this phrase often, and it helped because we thought we were making the right decisions based on their preferences and personality. But unfortunately, these three loved ones would not talk about death or make decisions regarding their final wishes.

I went to three of these awful meetings where I sat there bleary-eyed, holding back my tears, trying to keep it together so that I could help with the process. I can still remember what I felt. I remember it was hot in the room, crowded with all of my family members, that the funeral parlors had a particular smell, and I remember feeling so overwhelmed and barely able to function. When a death occurs to a loved one, you are exhausted, emotionally drained, in crisis mode, and unable to think clearly – a situation that is not conducive to good decision-making. If you have been through this before, you know how difficult it is to deal with these final arrangements when there is nothing in place. There are so many decisions that need to be made. It's an overwhelming process.

When my father passed away, my family chose the cemetery where my grandmother was buried. We chose cremation because his mother was cremated. My dad was the type of person who would never talk about death or anything associated with it. The decisions we made were purely based on speculation, and most sentences started with "Dad would want this" or "I think that Dad would be happy if…" The speculation continued and we muddled through this difficult time the best we could.

The same thing happened with my mother and my sister. We had no clue what either of them would want. We made decisions based on our gut feelings. Each time we made a decision, I remember thinking that I wished we had some written instructions. Unfortunately, there was no guide, and we had to do the best we could. In the end, I think we made the decisions they would have wanted. But no one should have to go through that.

The reason you should plan this area of your life is that it will help your family and loved ones through one of the most difficult times of their lives. Having clear instructions will ensure that your wishes are followed, and it will take the guesswork and some of the stress out of the moment. If your loved ones have instructions, they will not feel guilty that they have made the wrong decision. If possible, it is a good idea to pay for this expense beforehand to alleviate any additional monetary stress on your family.

It makes me feel so sad when I see a family having a car wash to raise money for funeral expenses. If funds are not available to take care of final wishes, this adds a tremendous amount of stress on your family to come up with the money. It is a good idea to pre-pay for these services or purchase a final expense plan that covers these expenses. The added bonus is that it will be cheaper to purchase it earlier rather than later because of inflation.

If you purchase a pre-need plan, you will also want to find out what your plan covers if you die in another state or overseas.

If you plan your final wishes beforehand, your family and loved ones can concentrate on grieving instead of enduring the stress of grieving while making a myriad of difficult decisions.

In the following section, the two main details of death will be reviewed. They are divided into two categories – the physical details and the emotional details. We will discuss many options, and there is a checklist at the end of the chapter to help you organize your wishes.

PHYSICAL DETAILS OF DEATH

The first set of choices have to do with the physical details of death. These are the practical matters: whether you prefer a burial, cremation, a green burial, or some other option. These types of services can be purchased beforehand, which is called pre-need planning.

Pre-need planning can be difficult to think about. Personally, I purchased a pre-need plan a few years ago, and it was difficult for me – even though I work in a profession that plans for death and dying. I purchased this plan for my loved ones. I do not want them to speculate about my wishes or feel guilty about whether they made the right decisions.

Cremation

Cremation has become a more common option over the years because of changing attitudes and acceptance. If you have decided on cremation, you'll need to decide what you want done with your cremated remains.

Some individuals want a niche at a cemetery, so their loved ones have a place to go to leave flowers or other mementos. A niche is a paid space at a cemetery where the remains are kept inside an urn. Some cemeteries have niches in stone walls; others have glassed-in or "open" niches for your loved ones to add mementos and pictures around the urn. Depending on the location, there may be other options available.

Other clients prefer to have their remains scattered at a special place or at sea. If you are planning on having your loved ones scatter your remains in a particular location, you will need to research whether local law allows the scattering of remains there and whether permission or a permit is required.

Willed-Body Program

Another option is the whole-body donation. Many medical schools allow the donation of your entire body, and medical students use it to study the body and the effect of disease. This donation provides medical students with an opportunity to learn.

If you decide you want to participate in a willed-body program, you will need to submit the proper forms to the medical school of your choice. After the documents are submitted, the medical school will confirm receipt of the forms and provide a phone number for your agent to call when you pass away. Some medical schools require that this document is notarized or witnessed.

Upon your death, the institution will arrange for the transportation of the remains. Some medical schools will only pay for transportation of the body for a specified number of miles. If you are considering this option, you will want to find out the process and the specific details of the program you are considering.

You should also find out what will happen with the remains after the students have completed their coursework. Based on my research, many medical schools will cremate the remains, at no charge. Oftentimes, you can designate an authorized representative to pick up the cremated remains, or there may be an option to authorize the medical school to bury the remains.

If you sign up for the willed-body program, it is important for you to keep a copy of the consent form and the contact information for the medical school in your essential-information file. This should be accessible by your loved ones so they know whom to call when the time comes.

Green Burial

Another option is a green burial. A green burial does not require embalmment. The body is placed in a non-toxic and biodegradable casket or shroud. It is then buried in a designated area and may contain a marker. This is a more recent option, and may or may not be available in the state where you live.

Cryogenics

As technology advances, some clients are deciding to opt for cryogenic preservation. This is the process whereby your body is frozen upon death. It is kept at a facility where it is maintained at a constant temperature until, theoretically, scientific advances make it possible for your body to be revived so you can resume living. There are various facilities in the country that offer this service, and oftentimes they will require a certain amount of money earmarked to pay for the ongoing cost. It is common to use life insurance to pay for this service.

Burial

If you choose the option of a burial, it is helpful to outline the details.

The first set of questions pertain to the details of the service. Do you want an open casket or not? Prior to the funeral or memorial, do you want a rosary or prayer service? All of these details can easily be documented so your family and loved ones will not have to make these decisions and then be forced to agonize over whether they did what you would have wanted.

The second question is where you want to be buried. Many clients decide to pre-purchase cemetery property so their family doesn't have to locate a place for their burial.

There are various options for burial. Some individuals purchase a plot in the ground or in a mausoleum. Some families choose to purchase several plots at the same time. If you do, you will want to determine who will be buried in which plot. It is advisable to document these plans and keep a copy of the contract and any other pertinent information in your essential-information file.

At the end of the chapter is a detailed checklist for your use.

EMOTIONAL DETAILS OF DEATH

The emotional details are matters concerning your wishes for your funeral or memorial. The emotional details of death reflect the way your life is honored, and it helps your family and loved ones to start the healing process.

When I discuss this with clients, most have a general idea of what they would or would not want. Some want grand affairs, while others want low-key services.

What are the details that are important to you? Are there particular religious traditions you want followed? Are there other types of remembrances or ceremonies you would like? While this may be one of the most difficult things to imagine, and certainly something that no one likes to think about, I usually start the discussion by asking clients about other memorial services or funerals they have attended. This is a good starting point to help them narrow down what they liked or didn't like. This may help you to start the process of discovering your preferences.

As with everything, people have preferences, and a little planning in this area can go a long way. Leaving instructions and, better yet, paying for these services ahead of time will ensure that your family have less stress and uncertainty.

After you have decided on the type of service, there will be other details you may want to consider. Following is a list of common considerations:

- Eulogy – Whom do you want to give the eulogy?
- Obituary – Do you want an obituary? If so, what would you like it to say? Are there favorite pictures you would like used?

- Music – Is there particular music you would like played? Are there hymns you would like played at the church, and different songs played at the reception?
- What poems or other readings would you like read?
- Flowers – Do you want flowers sent, or a donation to a particular charity in lieu of flowers?
- Program – What type of program would you like?
- Are there any other details you would like to include?

This is just a sample list of details to consider; there may be additional items you'll want to add. At the end of the chapter is a more detailed checklist.

HOW AND WHERE TO ORGANIZE THIS INFORMATION

In your advance healthcare directive or living will, you may want to document your final wishes. Having this information in your document will give your family and loved ones clear instructions.

If you have pre-paid for these services, be sure to organize the contracts.

There are two different services that are typically pre-paid. If you have pre-paid for cremation or for the cost to embalm your body, keep this contract in a place where your family can access it. Pre-paying for a burial plot or a niche for your cremated remains involves the purchase of cemetery property. You will have a contract specifying the location of your final resting spot.

If one or both of these services have been paid for, you should make sure your family knows this information and knows where to access these documents. I recommend keeping copies of the contract and any additional instructions in your essential-information file. I also recommend keeping a digital copy of this information.

Thinking about your final wishes is a difficult task. It is something that seems depressing and difficult. Over the years, I have noticed that clients who have planned and paid for their final wishes leave their family in a better place. Their families can concentrate on grieving instead of grieving while making arrangements. These families feel relieved that their loved one's wishes are followed, and they don't have to guess what their family member wanted. These families don't have guilt or uncertainty about whether they made the right decision. After a client passes away and I meet with their trustee, invariably when the trustee is speaking about the service, they are so grateful that they know what their loved one wanted and did not have to agonize over the decisions.

While I know it is difficult, I encourage you to think about what you want, and start making these arrangements now. I can tell you from personal experience that wrapping up this loose end is a tremendous benefit for your family. It will also give you peace of mind knowing that your wishes will be followed, and you have alleviated some of the stress for your family and loved ones.

☑ STEP 6
FINAL WISHES CHECKLIST

1. Physical details of death

    a. How do you wish for your remains to be handled?

        i. Burial

        ii. Cremation

        iii. Green burial

        iv. Cryogenic preservation

        v. Willed-body donation

    b. If applicable, have you pre-paid for these arrangements? If so, include a copy of the contract and proof of payment in your essential-information accordion file.

    c. What is your desired final resting place?

    d. Have you pre-purchased a burial plot, niche, or some other type of cemetery property? If so, provide the name and contact information of the cemetery. Also include a copy of the contract.

   e. If you choose to have your remains scattered, you may want to leave specific information your desired resting place. Also, you should conduct research whether a permit or other arrangements are required.

2. Emotional details of death

   a. Do you wish to have a service? If so, where will the service be held? Do you prefer a particular priest, pastor, or rabbi to perform the service? If so, you should provide his or her contact information.

   b. If you will have a traditional burial, do you want the casket at the service? If so, do you want an open casket? At the service, who would be your pallbearers?

   c. Do you want flowers, and if so, what kind? If not, would you prefer a donation to a particular charity or organization?

   d. Do you want particular music played?

e. Do you want particular poems, passages, or quotations read?

f. Are there particular pieces of music you want played?

g. Prior to the service, do you want a viewing? Who should be invited to the viewing – only close family members, or friends as well? Do you want a rosary service? Do you want any other pre-memorial or funeral services?

h. Do you wish to have a fraternal, military, or service organization present?

i. If you are a veteran, do you want the flag draped or folded? And to whom would you like the flag presented?

j. Do you want an obituary? If yes, is there a particular picture you would like used? What would you like the obituary to say? In what newspaper(s) should the obituary be printed? Do you also want an online remembrance page?

k. Are there any other special requests?

3. Managing this information

    a. Is this information managed digitally or are there physical copies? Have you told your family how to access this information?

    b. If you have pre-paid for these services, where are your contracts located? Can your family easily access this information?

STEP 6 – NOTES AND ACTION ITEMS

- [ ] _____
- [ ] _____
- [ ] _____
- [ ] _____
- [ ] _____
- [ ] _____
- [ ] _____
- [ ] _____
- [ ] _____

STEP 7

Create a Family Archive and Leave a Lasting Legacy

For many of my clients, one of their most important estate planning goals is to communicate their values and their life story. Many clients want future generations to know who they were, to have knowledge about their lives, their values, and what was important to them. This is often described, in broad terms, as a legacy.

Regardless of the term used, the notion is the same. The most common way to pass information to future generations is by utilizing pictures, videos, and writings.

This is particularly important for future generations that you will not meet in person. Through the process of completing this step, you will ensure that future generations will know who you were and what was important to you.

I decided to add this step while watching the news one night. There was a story about a couple who had lost everything in a flood. Their home was destroyed. The bottom floor of their home was under several feet of water. But the losses they kept talking about were the photographs and home movies that were destroyed. Understandably, they were devastated. By completing this step, you will avoid a situation where you lose your archives or deprive future generations of this information by not preparing.

Archiving is a personal decision, and how you choose to archive this information will depend on your preferences. There is no correct way to create a family archive; this is up to your imagination. In the past it's been common to create scrapbooks, but there are so many other alternatives in this day and age. Some of the most common items archived are photographs, videos, and mementos, but you can also include letters and messages to future generations.

Photographs

Nowadays, most of our photographs are already on our phones or tablets. But what would happen to your photographs if you lost your phone or tablet or it was no longer working? Keeping these files on the cloud or a media data service will ensure that these photographs are protected and available for those you would like to allow access.

With older photographs, you may want to consider scanning them. My mom loved to take pictures. I remember going with her to pick them up from the drugstore. There was much anticipation when you picked them up; sometimes they turned out well, other times not. My mom captured so many wonderful moments in these photographs that I still enjoy. She would invariably order two sets for every roll of film, and this resulted in mountains of photographs to review after my mom passed away.

It was a long, arduous process to catalog, scrapbook, and scan them. Part of the process of creating a family archive is gathering all of these photographs and organizing them in a way that makes sense to you. Some clients like to organize them by the individual family members, while others like to organize them by the decade or time period.

I created boxes for each time period and labeled them by year. I then reviewed the pictures in each box and determined whether I would scan them, create a scrapbook page, or throw them away. This part of the process can be difficult because, if you are like me, you may want to keep all of the photographs.

Everyone's personal preference varies, but I ended up throwing away duplicate photographs or pictures that were of poor quality; there were many where there was a thumb in the picture or the heads were cut off, etc. With others, I decided to scan them and organize them online. And there were some photographs that were so special to me that I scanned them and also put the physical copies in a scrapbook. Adding a caption or notes underneath the photograph in your handwriting is a special touch. You may have photographs that are so special to you that you keep them in your wallet or purse. Remember to scan these and/or make copies in case you lose your wallet.

I have a difficult time throwing away old photographs. For me, it's special to look at the original photograph.

Of course, this depends on your personal preference. While sorting through photographs, it can be helpful to work through this process with a family member or friend. You can help each other sort through the photographs, and have a lot of fun at the same time! It's a great opportunity for sharing stories and learning about each other.

Videos

With modern technology, it's now easy to store videos and share them with people of your choosing. But even for older videos on reels of film, you have options for permanent storage.

My mom was the photographer, but my dad liked to shoot videos. We had multiples reels of video that were quickly degrading, so my sister, Jill, arranged to have them digitized. We watched it together and had a great time. These videos were shared with each family member. If you have film that is degrading, you can digitize it, so it is not lost.

Letters, Documents, and Mementos

Other special items may include handwritten letters, notes and mementos. These types of items are a wonderful reminder of those we love. By preserving these items, the person who wrote the letter or owned the memento is remembered for generations to come. It's common to have family stores that have been passed down, but memories fade and information and stories can easily be lost if not documented.

I remember finding little notes after my mother and father passed away – even something as mundane as a shopping list was special to me. Seeing my loved one's handwriting was wonderful. Each one I found felt like a treasure.

In my archive, I've also included documents and letters that have a special significance. You may want to archive your relatives' naturalization or immigration documents, school records, identification cards, documents related to the purchase of the family home, or any other document that hold significance in your family history.

Some of the most precious things that many clients have are mementos or heirlooms such as special pieces of jewelry, artwork, furniture, or other collectibles. These types of items are often passed down from generation to generation. In your archive, you may want to include a picture of such items and an explanation of why they are important.

Genealogy

If you have genealogy records, you may want to have a system for organizing it and sharing it with family members. Depending on your preferences, you may wish to have this information in digital or paper format.

Similarly, if you have done an online DNA test, you will want to keep these reports in your archives, as well.

INFORMATION ABOUT YOUR CHILDREN

Birthdays

I love birthdays and the act of commemorating them. They are a wonderful time to remember how special a person is to you and to be grateful that he or she is in your life.

When I was growing up, my mom kept a keepsake memory book for each of her children. It was a spiral-bound book that had a space for your school picture and writing prompts where you could fill in information about the year. After my mom passed away I found this book, and it is so special to me. It is in her handwriting and contains information about that year.

One thing that I think is a wonderful gift for your children – or anyone that you are particularly close to – is what I call keepsake letters. I like to write these on the person's birthday each year, and I handwrite them because it is more personal. I keep a book for each important person in my life, and on his or her birthday, I add a few pages commemorating that year. You can also add favorite pictures, ticket stubs from events, or any other item from a special event or items that represent a milestone. These can be anything of significance, such as graduation programs, awards or the like.

Keepsake letters are powerful, and special to those who receive them. It is a way of leaving specific information for them. After you pass away, this special book will provide comfort for him or her.

I know that it can be difficult to begin. Below are some sentence starters to help you get started.

- I love you because…
- The traits that I most admire about you are…
- The things that I hope you will remember about me are…
- My favorite memories with you are…
- I dream that you will have a life filled with…
- My hopes for you are…
- The things I wish I would have done differently are…
- I am sorry because…
- I was proud when you…

The act of writing it down is what is important. It does not matter whether the grammar and spelling are perfect – it's the sentiment and the use of your own words and voice that make these types of documents precious to your loved ones.

Along with the keepsake letters, it's a good idea to keep an updated information list for each of your minor children. This information can be invaluable if something happens to you and his or her guardian needs to step in. Some of the documents and information you may want to organize are listed below.

Vital Records

The items that you gathered in Step 1, such as birth certificates, social security cards, and passports should be placed in your essential information file. For each of your children, you should make sure that you have the originals and copies.

School Information

- School records: this may include progress reports, report cards, and any school work that you would like to keep for your child.

- Any details that might be helpful for the named guardian. You may want to include practical information on how to motivate them to finish their homework and their habits. It's also a good idea to include information on how much guidance they need to complete the homework. It's a nice touch to add information about their teachers and their friends at school.

- Medical Information
    - Allergies
    - Medications
    - Doctors
    - Dentists and orthodontists

- Personal habits and routines
    - Morning routines
    - Bedtime routines
    - Quirks

- Preferences
    - Favorite things to do
    - Favorite places to go
    - Foods they like and don't like
    - Things that make them happy
    - Favorite toys
    - Trends that they followed
    - Favorite vacations
    - Songs they love and their favorite bands
    - Movies they like and their favorite actors
    - Books they have enjoyed
    - Funny things they like to say

- Awards and activities
    - Awards – academic, sports, or other types of awards

- Extracurricular activities – extracurricular activities they participated in, and any additional information you would like to include about these activities.

Child Identification Kit

Complete a Child Identification Kit. The National Identification Program is a program that offers this service. They will place your child's fingerprints and other identifying information in a national database.

Ideally, you will want to update this list, at least once a year. An easy way to remember to create your Keepsake Letter and update your child's information is to set a yearly reminder. This letter to your child along with practical information about their essential details is practical and something your child will treasure.

This is the type of document that you and your child can review together over the years. It will bring back many happy memories for both of you. It can be handwritten or typed, whatever you feel comfortable doing. You can place these in a special book or folder – let your creativity flow! You'll be glad that you kept this information and updated it once a year. It's funny; we think that we'll remember all of these special things about our children, but as the years pass, so many things are easily forgotten.

The next question is the format of this information. Now, each of us have preferred ways of organizing information and pictures. One idea is to keep scrapbook pages and personalize it with this information. Or you may want to keep a binder for your child. Or it might be organized in files. It doesn't matter how you decide to organize this information; the important thing is that you do it.

If your children are minors, I suggest you tell your named guardians where you keep this information and how to access it, in case there is an emergency.

STORING FAMILY ARCHIVES

The final step is deciding how to store this information. You may decide to only maintain electronic versions or you may want to keep the actual pictures. As discussed earlier, you will want to sort the materials and then decide how to archive them. Depending on your preference, you may decide to keep the physical document of one item and an electronic version of another. With respect to your family archives, you will want to make decisions on how you want to organize these items. Taking this step now will ensure that future generations will have the opportunity to gain a deeper understanding of their family history and story.

CONCLUSION

Family archives is a subject that is often overlooked. It typically comes up when someone passes away and clients are looking for photographs or videos for the memorial. But it doesn't have to be that way. Why not take time now to organize this information and memories for future generations? Of all of the steps, this is the most creative one. You can create a set of memories that will be cherished for generations.

Now that you have finished family archives, let's move on to our final topic: emergency preparedness.

☑ STEP 7
FAMILY ARCHIVES CHECKLIST

1. Photographs

    a. Sort by individual, time period, or subject matter

    b. Decide what to do with them – purge, scrapbook, or scan?

2. Videos

    a. Transfer to a permanent medium?

    b. Share the videos?

3. Letters, documents, mementos

    a. Sort these items and add notes and information for each

4. Genealogy records

5. Keepsake letters

6. Information about your minor children

STEP 7 – NOTES AND ACTION ITEMS

- [ ] _____
- [ ] _____
- [ ] _____
- [ ] _____
- [ ] _____
- [ ] _____
- [ ] _____
- [ ] _____
- [ ] _____

STEP 8

Prepare an Emergency Plan and Gather Supplies

Congratulations! You have finished seven of the eight steps!

In our final step, we are going to discuss emergency planning and preparedness. This is an easy thing to overlook. But statistically, disasters can happen anytime or anywhere. It's easy to place this on the back burner, but we are periodically reminded when an emergency or disaster happens near us. Unfortunately, at that point, you will be scrambling to come up with a plan and it will cause you more stress. But, with a little bit of planning, gathering supplies, and organizing information, you will have peace of mind knowing that you have a plan in place.

The first step is determining the likelihood of certain types of emergency situations common to your geographic area. In some areas, the major threat may be hurricanes and flooding, while in other areas it may be wildfires or earthquakes. Preparing for these different types of emergencies will be similar, but your plans will need to be tailored for the types common to your region.

In my geographic area, one of the major threats are wildfires. Last year, my house was in the evacuation zone. I was terrified. I packed a few suitcases and the supplies for our pets, but quickly realized that space was limited.

I was forced to make decisions about what I would take with me. I realized which items were most important to me. I wasn't as concerned about pictures and the family archive because I have that digitized. Along with clothes, personal items, and emergency supplies, I packed a few sentimental items and knick-knacks. There were only a few things that were priceless to me, such as pieces of jewelry and some other small items.

Luckily, the fire did not reach our house, but it made me think about what items were truly irreplaceable to me.

At the time of the publication of this book, the latest threat was the Novel Coronavirus 19. Given the novelty of this disease, planning for this threat is evolving. As time passes, there will be additional types of threats that we will need to continue to plan for. Your emergency plan should continually evolve so you can prepare for new situations.

Regardless of the type of threat in your geographic area, pre-planning will keep your family protected.

The three steps to emergency planning are preparing a communication plan, gathering the necessary physical supplies, and organizing the pertinent information. In the following sections I will review these three areas. I encourage you to consult with government agencies, such as Ready√ and the Federal Emergency Management Agency (FEMA). These websites can provide you with more extensive information. Your local government agencies and community emergency-planning organizations are excellent sources of information, resources, and classes as well.

Information, Communication and a Plan

During or after an emergency, the first necessity is information. The federal government has instituted a system called the Integrated Public Alert and Warning System (IPAWS). Through this agency, emergency communications can be sent via text. These are called Wireless Emergency Alerts (WEAs) and can warn you of an imminent threat or alerts. There are Amber Alerts for children under eighteen years old who have been abducted or are in danger. There are Silver Alerts for missing adults over sixty years old who have a cognitive impairment, such as Alzheimer's disease. There are Golden Alerts for adults over eighteen years old who have a mental or cognitive impairment. These are automatic and there is no need to subscribe to the service.

We also have the Emergency Alert System (EAS). This is a national public warning system used to broadcast emergency alerts on television and radio. You have probably heard the periodic national emergency alert system tests on your television or radio station with a loud beeping sound and announcement.

There are also local emergency alert systems. These emergency alerts will send information to your cell phone, landline, or email about natural disasters such as fires, earthquakes, or severe weather. It can also provide information and instructions for what to do during a disaster. Typically, you need to subscribe to this service. You may want to conduct research about the emergency alert systems in your area. If you can't locate the information on how to subscribe, you can contact your local emergency planning office for further information.

These systems operate on national, state, and local levels to disseminate information needed by the public in case of an emergency.

After an emergency, there may be a need to call for help, if you are sick or injured. You will also want to make sure that your family and friends are safe. In this day and age, people naturally assume that they will use their cell phone. But what if the cell towers are down or overloaded?

You may want to consider obtaining a ham radio license through the Federal Communications Commission. In order to obtain a license, you are required to pass a test. This alternative form of communication allows you to get in touch with others if you're unable to use your cell phone. It can also be used to signal for help. You can even join one of the many volunteer organizations who use their ham radio skills to help first responders communicate information. Once you obtain your ham radio license, there are groups that provide training on how you can use your skills as a ham radio operator in emergency situations. My dad (W6SPA) was an avid ham radio operator and received the training necessary to assist in emergency situations. Having trained individuals with these skills is an important public service.

Finally, you will want to have a plan. A communication plan will ensure that you have decided who will be the central point of contact and who will be the alternate, in case the first point of contact cannot be reached. You may want to pick individuals living in different areas, just in case communications are not available in particular areas. You'll also want to have a plan for where you will meet in case of emergency.

Physical Supplies

You'll next need to gather the physical supplies for your emergency kit. The Federal Emergency Management Agency (FEMA) provides lists of recommended supplies. This list appears below. I have included additional items that I think may be helpful.

- Water — One gallon of water per person for a period of three days
- Food — A three-day supply of non-perishable food. Be sure to include a manual can opener if you have canned food in your emergency kit.
- Flashlight and batteries, as well as an LED headlamp
- Solar powered flashlight
- Solar-powered cell phone charger
- A battery-powered or hand-crank radio, a NOAA weather radio, and extra batteries
- Whistle and flares
- Paper or plastic cups, plates, utensils, and paper towels
- Medical supplies — An up-to-date first-aid manual, bandages, cut cleaner, gauze pads, medical tape, antiseptic, aspirin, hydrogen peroxide, tweezers, scissors, cold packs, thermometer, plastic gloves, and any other types of medical supplies that may be useful
- Dust masks
- Plastic sheeting and duct tape, in case you need to shelter in place
- Cash and coins
- At least a one-week supply of your prescription medications
- An extra pair of eyeglasses, and, if you wear contacts, an extra pair of contacts and contact-lens solution

- If you have a hearing aid, an extra hearing-aid battery
- Sleeping bag or warm blanket for each person
- Change of clothing for each person
- Hygiene items – moist towelettes, washcloths, toothpaste and toothbrushes, dental floss, soap, and any other hygiene items that may be useful
- Large garbage bags
- Personal power station – They sell ones that have power plugs and USB hookups. These power stations can also be used to charge a car battery or put air in a tire.
- Wrench or pliers to turn off utilities
- Water treatment kit
- Matches in a waterproof container and a lighter

We never know where, when, or what type of emergency will occur. For this reason, it is a good idea to store emergency supplies in several different places. Typically you will have the largest supply of emergency items at your home, but you should also keep emergency kits at your place of work and in your car. For your car in particular, you will want to include a first-aid kit, flares, jumper cables, extra clothes and shoes, and a supply of food and bottled water.

Personal Information

The third need is personal information. In previous chapters we discussed the organization of all of your vital records, estate planning records, financial records, health information, and family archives. The organization of this information serves two purposes.

The first is to provide your family with crucial information when you die or if you become incapacitated, and the second is to ensure that you will have the needed information in the event of an emergency. Having this information at your fingertips will make emergency situations less stressful.

For that reason, I suggest creating the essential-information file. This could be a plastic accordion file, binder, or portable box that you can grab in the event of an emergency. The essential-information file should contain dividers and folders so information is organized by each step. Ideally, this would be the type of item that can easily be transported. Keep it in a place that is easily accessible so you can grab it quickly if necessary.

In my home, we call it the "important box." It is a file box with a handle that has files for each of the steps. My family knows where the box is located, and they know that they should grab it in an emergency.

SPECIAL PLANNING SITUATIONS

Children

You will want to review the emergency plan and policies at the schools where your children attend. Make sure you know the school's policies and procedures beforehand. You should also talk to your children about the emergency plan. Without scaring them, you should tell them where they should go or where to meet you if there is an emergency. It is also a good idea to coordinate with other parents and have a plan for how you can help each other's children, if necessary.

Seniors and People With Disabilities

If you are caring for a senior citizen or a person who is disabled, you may want to consider organizing items specific to their needs. For example, if your loved one uses a motorized wheelchair, you should obtain an extra battery charger, along with extra batteries. You can also keep an extra non-motorized, lightweight wheelchair to use in the event that the motorized wheelchair won't work.

If your loved one uses oxygen, make sure that you have a sufficient supply. If medical or assistive devices are used, gather additional battery chargers for each of these items.

For those individuals who have service animals, create an emergency plan for them. This will include sufficient food, water, and other necessary supplies for the service animal.

The city, town, or county where you live may have an emergency registry. This is a registry that alerts governmental officials of the addresses of disabled individuals. It puts emergency personnel on notice that particular households may need emergency services first.

Pets – Household and Large Animals

When considering an emergency-preparedness plan, it is important to remember to plan for your pets. Depending on the type of pets you have, your plan will need to be tailored to meet their specific needs.

You should have a picture of each pet along with their identification information. You may also want to include a picture with you and your pet. If you are separated from your pets, you can use these pictures for identification purposes. You should already have this information organized from Step 2 – Estate Planning.

If your animal has a microchip, make sure that your contact information is up-to-date.

For your dog, cat, or other domestic animals, you will want to have the following items:

- At least three days of food in easy-to-transport containers
- A food dish and water bowl
- Cat litter
- Dog or cat toys
- Medications and information on dosage
- An extra collar and leash
- A first-aid kit for your pet
- A pet carrier for each of your pets

In my pet crates, I keep food, extra medications, collars and leashes, and first-aid supplies. This way, if there is an emergency, I merely need to put my animals in their carriers and I am ready to take them to safety.

For birds, reptiles, and fish, you may want to have the following items:

- For fish aquariums, make sure the aquarium is bolted to the wall studs or placed on the floor, as this will decrease the possibility of the aquarium falling over.

- For reptiles and birds, you will want to have a cage, cage cover, food, water bowls, newspaper, medication, first-aid items, toys and treats, veterinarian information, and any other type of necessary equipment for each reptile or bird.

- For large animals and livestock, you will need to determine where you can take your animals in the event of an emergency. You may want to contact the local fairgrounds or other facilities in your area to determine their emergency policy.

You will want to know where you can house your pets safely if an evacuation is necessary. You may want to coordinate your emergency plan with your friends or neighbors. By creating a plan together, you can have an agreement on how you can help each other. As a bonus, it is a great way to meet your neighbors, if you haven't already!

You will also need proper identification information for each of your animals. Keep a list of their branding, ear-tags, and microchips in their separate files. Of course, as discussed in earlier steps, you may consider keeping this information on a USB located in your essential-information file, as well as on a cloud-based service. If your animals become separated from you, you will need proof that they belong to you.

Other items you may want to have are feed for three days, ropes and halters, wire cutters, water buckets, and any other items that your large animals may need in case of an emergency.

For all of your large animals and livestock, you should have a file containing their current vaccinations, medical history, medication requirements, and special dietary requirements.

CONCLUSION

Unfortunately, most individuals have an ad hoc system for planning for an emergency. In other words, when the emergency happens, they make a plan. This is not an efficient method and can lead to undesirable and even tragic situations.

If you take the time to plan now, you will have a checklist and supplies ready when an emergency happens. While it will be scary and uncertain during an emergency, this planning will help you and your family to be a bit more calm when the unexpected happens.

☑ STEP 8
EMERGENCY PREPAREDNESS CHECKLIST

1. Communication and a plan

2. Physical supplies

3. Information

4. Special planning situations

    a. Children

    b. Seniors

    c. Individuals with disabilities

    d. Animals

STEP 8 – NOTES AND ACTION ITEMS

- [ ] _____
- [ ] _____
- [ ] _____
- [ ] _____
- [ ] _____
- [ ] _____
- [ ] _____
- [ ] _____
- [ ] _____

Wrapping Up Loose Ends: Continuing the Journey

Thank you for joining me on this journey. I hope you feel like you are prepared both for the things you know will happen and for the things that may happen. This type of organization and document management will bring you so much peace of mind; now you don't need to worry as much when the unexpected happens.

More importantly, these steps will help your family and loved ones when an unexpected event occurs. If you are unable to communicate with them directly, these steps will give them the direction they need in a time that is already hard. I know the topics in the steps are difficult ones, and I suspect that some were much more difficult than others.

Throughout this book, you embarked on a journey encompassing many different areas of your life. While they may not seem related, the completion of these steps are related to your overall sense of well-being. The details you have thoughtfully organized create a base for a well-organized and prepared life.

When I meet with a grieving family who is mourning the loss of a loved one or dealing with their loved one being incapacitated, the stress on them is lessened if things have been planned, organized, and communicated.

This is not the time to be complacent or be on auto-pilot. Even though you have all of the steps completed, you should commit to reviewing this information on a yearly basis. You can enforce this accountability by merely writing or inputting a review date on your calendar. You will be surprised by how much more you will have to add each year. Depending on what occurs during the year, you may have more to add to particular steps.

When life events occur, you will want to reassess choices that may be applicable to that life event. As you acquire new assets, you will want to ensure that they are documented in your Step 3 storage system, and that you have titled them into your living trust, if applicable.

With that being said, it is impossible to prepare for every possible event that may occur. Just as an example, while I was in the process of editing this book, the COVID-19 pandemic happened. The idea that a pandemic would occur that would be on par with the pandemic of 1918 was inconceivable to me.

Nevertheless, having my personal information and steps completed gave me the peace of mind that I had prepared a roadmap for my family, if the worst thing happened.

I hope you have enjoyed this experience and that you feel better prepared for whatever may come next. Thank you again for taking this journey with me. I wish you the best of health, happiness, and wealth!

In gratitude,

Nancy

ACKNOWLEDGMENTS

"A single act of kindness throws out roots in all directions, and the roots spring up and make new trees."
Amelia Earhart

First and foremost, I dedicate this book to the memory of Vicky Michelis. She encouraged me to write this book – literally for years. Vicky was the type of person who had boundless energy and enthusiasm. She was taken from this world too early and I miss her. Vicky was a tireless advocate for ovarian cancer awareness and started the nonprofit Teal's Real to educate women about the signs and symptoms of this terrible disease so it can be detected as early as possible. Vicky was a wonderful friend and I was blessed to have her in my life.

Second, to my wonderful partner and friend, Jesse. Jesse is the type of person you want on your side. Jesse has an innovative, calm, and fun attitude toward life. I am so grateful to him.

Not only did Jesse help me with my business, but even his parents were strong supporters. I am grateful for all of the practical things they taught me, especially about selling and closing the deal. I had no idea when I started my law office that part of the business is sales. I am grateful to them for teaching me this and supporting me in my business endeavors.

To the memory of my mom and dad. There is not a day that goes by that I do not think of them. I didn't realize how smart my parents were until I became older and appreciated them. I am grateful to them for instilling a strong work ethic, and for teaching me to act with integrity, kindness, and respect.

To the memory of my sister, Barbara. She was the type of person who loved people unconditionally and was always your biggest fan. She was so full of life and had a warm heart for those who were part of her life. Barbara was willing to lend a helping hand to anyone. She had the most giving spirit of anyone I have ever known.

I am grateful to my niece, Sydney. She has so many of the same wonderful qualities as her mother. Sydney is intelligent, kind, generous, and fun. I am so proud of her and happy that Barbara's legacy of generosity and kindness lives on inside of her. The world certainly needs more of that these days.

This is in gratitude to my sisters, Susanne, Karen, Gail, and Jill. Faced with so much tragedy, we could have fallen apart and things could have gone sideways quickly. We faced these difficult times with love for each other and got through them together. I am grateful that we are able to come together as a family in the best of times and, more importantly, in the worst of times. I am incredibly proud to call them my sisters. They are role models and friends. This is in acknowledgment of my nieces, Leela, Ina, and Jessica, and my one nephew, Jason. I am incredibly proud that you have all turned into such amazing young people!

I want to acknowledge Kenyon, Walter, and Jude at the Santa Clara County Superior Court. They provided information that was particularly important for Step 1 – Vital Records. They work so hard and provide such an important service to the community. It is easy to take court clerks and those that work in the government for granted. They provide a vital service to our community and should be appreciated for their hard work.

A big thank-you to Maurice for teaching me to sail. So many life lessons can be learned on a sailboat, especially when sailing in the challenging conditions of the San Francisco Bay Area. It has taught me to continually see your destination on the horizon, but to make adjustments along the way. Here's to fair winds and calm seas!

Finally, I am grateful to all of my clients. Over the course of my career, I have learned so much from them. Living in the Bay Area, I have had the opportunity to meet with clients from every walk of life. Each story is unique and fascinating, and no two are alike. It is an honor and privilege to help them navigate and complete their estate planning.

ABOUT THE AUTHOR

Nancy Williamson is an attorney and founder of Four Seasons Estate Planning located in Sunnyvale, California. Nancy helps families navigate the complexities of estate planning and trust administration, and works to create solutions tailored to their specific needs.

She earned earned her J.D. degree from the University of the Pacific, McGeorge School of Law.

Nancy is the past president of the Santa Clara County Estate Planning Council, and past president of the Silicon Valley Chapter of the Society of Financial Service Professionals.

She obtained a Bachelor's Degree in Social Work from San Francisco State University. This experience provides her with a strong knowledge of family dynamics and uniquely equips her to help families with their estate planning needs.

Nancy enjoys volunteering in the community. She served two terms on the City of San Jose Senior Citizen Commission.

Nancy resides in San Jose, California. Her hobbies include sailing, gardening, and crafting.

LET'S WRAP UP LOOSE ENDS!

Are you a trusted advisor with clients that could benefit from this book or presentation?

For discounted bulk purchases of this book for your company, professional association, or conference, please email: nwilliamson@fourseasonsestateplanning.com

For additional resources, please visit: www.fourseasonsestateplanning.com

YouTube Channel
Four Seasons Estate Planning

Facebook
Four Seasons Estate Planning